RUN THE GAUNTLET

The Channel Dash 1942

KEN FORD

OSPREY PUBLISHING
Bloomsbury Publishing Plc

PO Box 883, Oxford, OX1 9PL, UK
1385 Broadway, 5th Floor, New York, NY 10018, USA
Email: info@ospreypublishing.com

Transferred to digital print on demand 2018

First published 2012
2nd impression 2012

Printed and bound in Great Britain

A CIP catalogue record for this book is available from the British Library

Print ISBN: 978 1 84908 570 0
PDF e-book ISBN: 978 1 84908 571 7
EPUB e-book ISBN: 978 1 78096 041 8

Page layout by Bounford.com
Index by Alison Worthington
Maps by Bounford.com
BEV by Alan Gilliland
Typeset in Sabon
Originated by United Graphics Pte., Singapore

The Woodland Trust
Osprey Publishing is supporting the Woodland Trust, the UK's leading woodland conservation charity, by funding the dedication of trees.

www.ospreypublishing.com
To find out more about our authors and books visit our website. Here you will find extracts, author interviews, details of forthcoming events and the option to sign-up for our newsletter.

IMPERIAL WAR MUSEUM COLLECTIONS

Many of the photos in this book come from the Imperial War Museum's huge collections which cover all aspects of conflict involving Britain and the Commonwealth since the start of the twentieth century. These rich resources are available online to search, browse and buy at **www.iwmcollections.org.uk** – In addition to Collections Online, you can visit the Visitor Rooms where you can explore over 8 million photographs, thousands of hours of moving images, the largest sound archive of its kind in the world, thousands of diaries and letters written by people in wartime, and a huge reference library. To make an appointment, call (020) 7416 5320, or email mail@iwm.org.uk.

Imperial War Museum: www.iwm.org.uk

CONTENTS

INTRODUCTION

On 22 January 1941, two German battlecruisers, the *Scharnhorst* and the *Gneisenau*, left Kiel harbour and set course for the northern waters around Iceland. Flying his flag on board *Scharnhorst*, Admiral Lütjens, then *Flottenchef* (Chief of Fleet) of the *Kriegsmarine* (German Navy), ordered his captains to wage war on merchant shipping in the north Atlantic, in a cruise that was without precedent. For the first time, Germany would use its capital ships to attack shipping lanes, whilst all the while seeking to avoid contact with heavy British warships.

Once out into the open ocean, the two warships prowled the desolate wastes, seeking unprotected convoys and lone merchantmen. Whenever a British battleship was sighted protecting a convoy, Lütjens' battlecruisers withdrew to find easier targets. They voyaged south into the shipping lanes off Africa and then northwards across Atlantic sea routes, sinking ships and spreading alarm amongst the British. They were refuelled by tankers and assisted by the presence in the Atlantic of other German warships, for the pocket battleship *Admiral Scheer* and the heavy cruiser *Admiral Hipper* were also out at sea. In just two months the two sister ships were able to sink 22 vessels amounting to almost 116,000 tons of shipping. After weeks on the rampage, mechanical defects started to appear, the most serious of which was within the boilers of the *Scharnhorst*. On 22 March, the two warships entered the safe harbour of Brest in north-west France after what had been a long and very successful sortie.

The French naval base at Brest was by this time very much a German port. Almost the whole of its personnel had been moved there from Wilhelmshaven, along with their heavy equipment. Brest had become an established northern refuge for Nazi ships operating in the Atlantic. Its facilities were now directed towards making the two capital ships ready for an even greater raid into northern waters, for it was planned that they would be joined by the most powerful vessel in the German fleet, the newly commissioned battleship *Bismarck*.

At the start of World War II, a nation's power was measured by the number of capital ships in its navy. These large vessels – battleships, battlecruisers and aircraft carriers – were tremendously expensive to build and to keep operational, but the power they could wield through their massive guns meant that realistically they could only be countered by other equally formidable ships. Leading the world's surface fleets was Britain's Royal Navy, with its 15 battleships and battlecruisers in service in 1939. Most of these were dated, for only two of them had been built after the Great War. During the next five years of the conflict, five new *King George V* types were constructed in an attempt to keep pace with the new capital ships being built by the German *Kriegsmarine*.

Germany was a late starter in this particular area of the arms race, for after the Great War it was restricted by international agreement to building warships of less than 10,000 tons. It did produce what were termed '*panzerschiffe*' (pocket battleships), such as the *Graf Spee*, but these were in reality little more than heavy cruisers. When the war began, Germany had in service just two modern capital ships: the *Scharnhorst* and the *Gneisenau*; two other new and even more powerful vessels, the *Bismarck* and the *Tirpitz*, were under construction.

The *Scharnhorst* and the *Gneisenau* were built with the armoured plating of a battleship, and able to withstand a great deal of punishment, but were armed with 11in (28cm) guns rather than the more usual 15in (38cm) weapons found on battleships. The weight saved by adopting the lighter guns resulted in a much faster top speed, enabling the vessels to be more powerful than any other warship with lesser armament, and yet they would be quick

The *Gneisenau* as it was before the war in 1939. Later modifications provided the battlecruiser with a 'clipper' bow that enhanced its already powerful appearance to an even greater degree. (IWMHU 1043)

The *Scharnhorst*, the sister ship of the *Gneisenau*. Vizeadmiral Ciliax raised his flag in the *Scharnhorst* for Operation *Cerberus*, but was forced to change ships during the voyage after the battlecruiser hit a mine off the coast of Holland. (IWM HU1042)

enough to escape from any enemy ship with larger guns. They were both around 32,000 tons with a top speed of 32 knots (This type of capital ship was termed a battlecruiser by the British, although the German insisted on seeing them as pure battleships (*Schlachtschiffe*). They were built primarily as commerce raiders, for they would be at a great disadvantage if ever compelled to fight a fleet action against the giants of the Royal Navy, as was demonstrated by the demise of the *Scharnhorst* later in the war.

Just the presence of the two battlecruisers in Brest acted as a constant threat to Britain's Atlantic sea lanes without the warships ever having to leave harbour. The danger of their suddenly setting sail and disappearing into the Atlantic put every convoy at risk and inevitably tied up capital ships that could be put to better use. The chance that they might put in an unexpected appearance amongst the slow merchantmen of a convoy, protected by just destroyers and the occasional 6in-gunned cruiser, filled the Admiralty with great anxiety. It was one thing to guard convoys from U-boats with anti-submarine frigates and destroyers, but quite another to have to allocate a valuable battleship to watch over them. There were just not enough of these great leviathans to go around. It was clear that something had to be done to eliminate the enemy battlecruisers at their berths in Brest as quickly as possible. The Admiralty now looked to the Royal Air Force (RAF) to help it out.

THE WARSHIPS AT BREST

Six days after the *Scharnhorst* and *Gneisenau* had entered Brest, their presence there was discovered on 28 March by photo-reconnaissance aircraft of the RAF. The *Scharnhorst* was berthed at the torpedo station along the open quayside of the Rade Abri, with the *Gneisenau* a few hundred yards away in the west dry dock. Steps were immediately taken to carry out bombing raids on the ships before the anti-aircraft defences became too formidable.

On the 30–31 March, Bomber Command dispatched 109 aircraft to Brest, 101 of which successfully made an attack. They dropped 132 tons of bombs on the port with little appreciable effect on the battlecruisers, although a number of the ships' companies were killed in their billets in the town. Returning aircrews reported they had encountered heavy flak from about 40 light guns along the waterfront. There was also more flak from guns located on the promontories to the north, south and west of Brest, as well as large concentrations of searchlights. This firepower was, however, only the start of German preparations to defend the ships, for by 24 August the flak defences of Brest had increased to 333 weapons, made up of 100 heavy, 84 medium and 149 light anti-aircraft guns.

The very first bombing attack made by the RAF demonstrated to the Germans that the ships had been discovered. Samples of shrapnel found after the raid showed that the bombs used were not just high-explosive, but contained a large number of armour-piercing types. It was clear that the bombers were not carrying out a straightforward raid on the docks, but were specifically after the warships. The next day aircraft from Bomber Command were back again. Four more raids followed over the ensuing five days.

The two battlecruisers had been at sea for eight straight weeks and each was in need of an overhaul and refit. Inspection of the *Scharnhorst* showed that the prolonged voyage had resulted in quite severe defects within its boilers. The ship's engineers estimated that it would take at least ten weeks to put matters straight. The *Gneisenau* had fared a little better and required only minor repairs to make it ready for sea again. All the work was to be carried out by German dockyard workers, for the local

French equivalents were banned from the vessels and their immediate surroundings. The Germans knew that the French Resistance had agents in the port and took great steps to keep all information useful to the British away from them.

On 5 April, *Gneisenau* was taken out of dry dock and moored to a buoy in the Rade Abri near La Mole. The next day, as chance would have it, aircraft from Coastal Command mounted a raid. Four Beaufort torpedo-bombers were sent from their base at St Eval to strike at the enemy ships. Three failed to make contact, but the fourth, flown by Flying Officer Kenneth Campbell, put in a determined attack. Campbell brought his aircraft in low over the water through a barrage of anti-aircraft fire to release his torpedo at close range. His projectile ran straight and true and exploded against the rear of the *Gneisenau*, wrecking the starboard propeller and its shaft. The sound of the explosion was drowned out by a simultaneous detonation as Campbell's aircraft, hit by flak, burst into flames and crashed into the water. All three of its crew were killed instantly.

The battlecruiser had been struck by what could have been a knock-out blow and immediately started to take on water. It soon began to list heavily. Fortunately for the crew, the vessel was in sheltered waters and a salvage boat quickly came alongside and began pumping water out of the stricken warship, whilst the men on board struggled to stabilize it. The next day it returned to the dry dock for repairs. Close inspection showed that the *Gneisenau* would be out of action for six months. Campbell's heroic action had given the Admiralty breathing space. At least one of the ships would not be putting to sea in the near future. For his valour in pressing home the attack, Campbell was awarded a posthumous Victoria Cross.

The heavy cruiser *Prinz Eugen* in port in Germany. The cruiser saw a good deal of action during World War II and ended its days as a target ship for the Americans in their atomic bomb tests in the Pacific. (IWM MH 30195)

Night after night, the RAF continued to mount raids on the battlecruisers. On 10 April, the *Gneisenau* was hit again. Three bombs struck the ship, killing more than 50 seamen and setting fire to its superstructure and other parts of the vessel. One of its magazines had to be flooded to prevent the spread of the flames. It was clear that these night attacks would continue while the ships were in port, but there was no chance of their putting to sea again until the repairs had been made. The Germans decided to make Brest into a fortress, increasing the number of anti-aircraft defences, moving fighter aircraft onto nearby airfields and installing smoke generators to shield the port whenever an incoming bombing raid was detected.

At that same time, away to the north in the sheltered anchorage of Bergen in Norway, the newly commissioned *Bismarck* was now readying itself for action. A plan had originally been made for a combined sortie into the North Atlantic with the two battlecruisers. This plan was now not possible. The damage to the Brest ships resulted in their being confined to the dockyard for between three and six months whilst repairs were completed. Even then their seaworthiness would depend on not suffering further damage by the RAF. The *Kriegsmarine* leadership was, however, still anxious that the *Bismarck* should be used as soon as possible against Britain's merchant fleet. The original plan would now have to be changed. It was decided that the *Bismarck* would still make its sortie into the Atlantic, but would be escorted by just the heavy cruiser, the *Prinz Eugen*.

The two warships set sail on 20 May 1941. Their departure was quickly detected by the British, and the Admiralty despatched ships of the Home Fleet from Scapa Flow to intercept them near the Denmark Straits off Iceland. On 24 May the battleship *Prince of Wales* and the battlecruiser *Hood* engaged the *Bismarck* and its escort in an action that demonstrated the great power of the German warship. HMS *Hood* was sunk and the *Prince of Wales* badly damaged. The *Bismarck* then made to escape into the open waters of the Atlantic, but was continually tracked by British cruisers and destroyers.

Try as they might, the two German warships could not shake off the shadowing force. British radar was so effective that each time they disappeared into the mist and rain, they remained visible on radar screens. With the German ships' exact location in the Atlantic known, other Royal Navy capital ships were sent from Gibraltar to intercept. In the meantime, the carrier *Victorious* was diverted to attack the *Bismarck*. Swordfish aircraft from 825 Squadron, led by Lieutenant-Commander Eugene Esmonde, made a night attack. They came at the battleship at low level, flying just above the wave tops, and were able to release their torpedoes at a range of less than 1,100yds. *Bismarck* was hit amidships. The explosion was not enough to sink it, but it was severe enough to slow it down considerably.

During the next three days the German battleship was attacked by torpedo-firing destroyers and aircraft from the newly arrived carrier *Ark Royal* which slowed the vessel down even more. Finally, the battleships *King George V* and the *Rodney* reached the position of the *Bismarck* and engaged her. The fight was a protracted one-sided slogging match. Out-numbered, out-manoeuvred and out-gunned, the damaged German battleship eventually

28 MARCH 1941

RAF aircraft identify *Scharnhorst* and *Gneisenau* in Brest

30–31 MARCH 1941

Start of RAF bombing raids against Brest

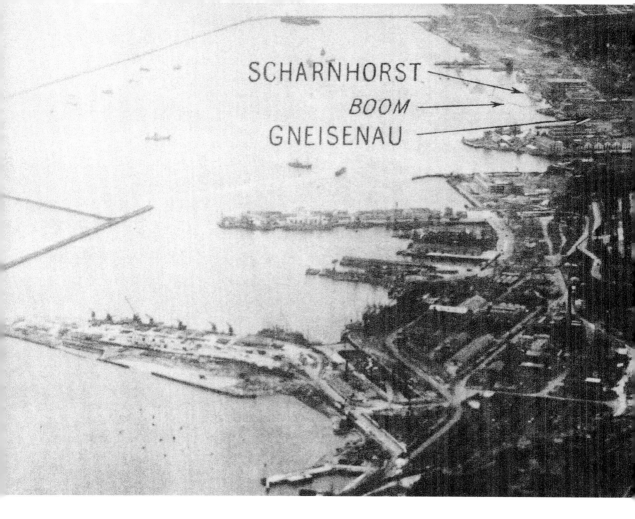

SCHARNHORST

BOOM

GNEISENAU

succumbed to the battering it received from shells of all calibres. The great guns of the British capital ships and smaller, but nonetheless effective, weapons of the cruisers reduced her to a wreck. The final *coup de grace* was struck by torpedoes fired from the cruiser *Dorsetshire*. At 1039hrs on 27 May, the *Bismarck*, the pride of the German *Kriegsmarine*, sank into the grey Atlantic Ocean.

Before this final action, the heavy cruiser *Prinz Eugen* had slipped away from the net that was closing around the German ships and disappeared into the wide Atlantic Ocean. The fate of the *Bismarck* had by then been sealed, and the heavy cruiser's presence could do little to avert the inevitable. Nothing more was heard of *Prinz Eugen* for several days, for it maintained radio silence to avoid detection by the British. A search was made for the cruiser by ships and reconnaissance aircraft, but it could not be found. Then, on 1 June, *Prinz Eugen* appeared out of an early morning mist at the harbour entrance to Brest – it had made its escape and had reached the safety of a German-held port. The *Prinz Eugen* was quickly brought into the dockyard and secured alongside one of the quays that lined the Rade Abri, joining the battlecruisers. Germany now had a complete battlefleet holed up in Brest.

Channel Dash Warship Specifications

Scharnhorst and *Gneisenau*	
Launched	1936
Tonnage	32,000 tons
Length	741ft (226m)
Beam	98ft (30m)
Main Armament	9 × 11in (28cm) guns
Secondary Armament	12 × 5.9in (15cm) guns
	14 × 4.1in (10.5cm) anti-aircraft guns
	16 × 1.45in (3.7 cm) anti-aircraft guns
	6 × 21in (53cm) torpedo tubes
Speed	32 knots
Crew	Approximately 1,900 officers and men
Prinz Eugen	
Launched	1938
Tonnage	10,000 tons
Length	697ft (212m)
Beam	72ft (21.8m)
Main Armament	8 × 8in (20cm) guns
Secondary Armament	12 × 4.1in (10.5cm) guns
	17 × 1.5in (4cm) anti-aircraft guns
	8 × 1.45in (3.7cm) anti-aircraft guns
	6 × 21in (53cm) torpedo tubes
Speed	32 knots
Crew	Approximately 1,600 officers and men

INITIAL STRATEGY

The demise of the *Bismarck*, and the manner in which the British were able to track and shadow the battleship in the Atlantic through their superior radar, led to a rethink of German naval strategy. There was a real danger that once a warship had been detected, the Royal Navy could monitor its movements and vector in an overwhelming force to annihilate it. The British had demonstrated that their powerful northern battlefleet, plus numbers of aircraft carriers, would eventually corner any German capital ship that chose to break out of European waters to attack the shipping lanes that fed Britain. Should the newly completed *Tirpitz* ever venture out into open waters, then its fate would in all probability be similar to that of its sister ship the *Bismarck*. The same could also be true of the battlecruisers in Brest; they might be fast and capable of disappearing into the open Atlantic for a while, but there was a great chance that they would eventually be found and brought to battle by an overwhelming force. Their role as commerce raiders would now have to be re-thought, as would that of the *Tirpitz*.

On 1 July, the RAF struck lucky. During a daylight raid on the docks at Brest, an armour-piercing bomb penetrated the thick steel plates of the *Prinz Eugen* and exploded in the vital command section of the ship. More than 40 of its crew were killed and many more injured. The damage was severe enough to put the warship out of action for three months. Three weeks after this mishap, on 23 July, the *Scharnhorst* was made ready for sea and left the port on an exercise bound for the smaller French harbour of La Pallice. During the 250-mile voyage, the warship tested its repaired boilers and practised firing its guns. In the sheltered waters off the coast, it worked up to a speed of over 30 knots without mishap. It looked as though *Scharnhorst* was ready to resume service once again.

This state of optimism did not last long, for the RAF had detected the movement. It appeared to the Admiralty as though the enemy ship was about to attempt a breakout into the Atlantic again. To counter such a possibility, a large bomber force was quickly assembled to attack the warship in La Pallice. The first raid was made at dusk whilst the ship was alongside, and

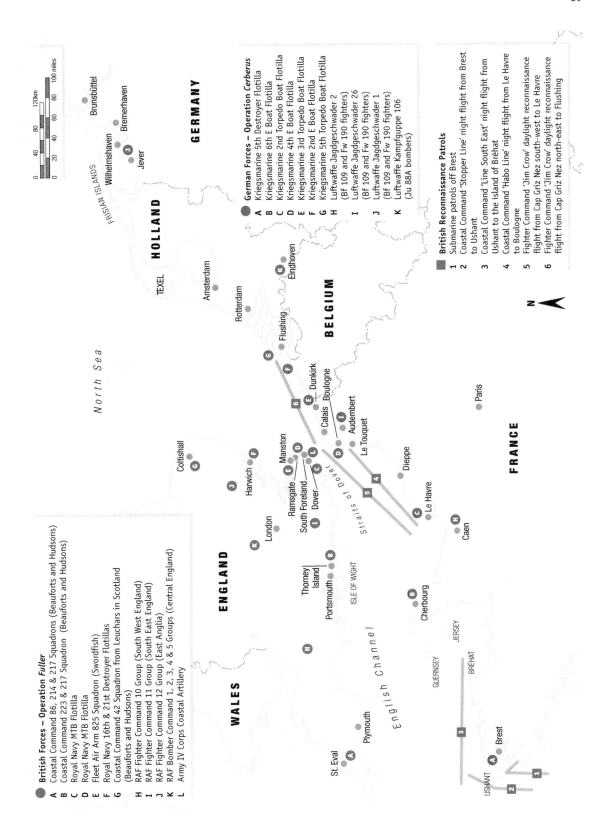

Forces engaged in Operations *Fuller* and *Cerberus*.

The heavy cruiser *Prinz Eugen* in dry dock in Brest. The warship is shrouded in camouflage netting in the hope of fooling British reconnaissance aircraft, but the location of the dry docks within the port had already been well recorded. (IWM HU35745)

one of the Stirling bombers scored a direct hit on the warship with an armour-piercing bomb. Further attacks were made again that night. The next day, a bomber fleet comprised of 84 Wellingtons, Hampdens and Flying Fortresses again attacked the ship. *Scharnhorst* was hit several more times and began taking on water. The crew managed to patch up the damage and reduce the list sufficiently for the warship to return to dry dock in Brest the next day. Now all three ships of the German battlefleet were immobilized as a result of RAF Bomber Command's actions. And still the raids continued.

The RAF returned to Brest by day and night well into the summer. The bombers attempted to score more hits on the three Nazi warships, but fighters, flak and fog generators made accurate bombing difficult. The raids did, however, cause casualties amongst the German crews and dock workers. The situation became so serious that service personnel were moved out of the port at night into barracks on the outskirts of the town. With the ships idle and with no immediate likelihood of their putting to sea, some of the crews were moved back to Germany and replaced by new recruits, who used the vessels as training ships whilst the repairs were made.

Hitler regarded all of his major vessels as a costly extravagance, especially the three ships stood in Brest. Certainly their existence was great for the Nazi propaganda machine, and their occasional victories were a cause for celebration, but they were expensive to maintain in both men and matériel at a time when the German war machine was starting to feel the strains of the new front that had opened up against the Soviet Union. There was also another aspect that troubled Hitler. Britain was making a number of raids on Norway and the dictator felt that the country could become a target for invasion. Hitler was convinced that Norway would prove to be a crucial 'zone of destiny' in the war and he needed to strengthen its defences.

Hitler reasoned that all of his capital ships and heavy cruisers should be based in Norway so that they might counter any invasion fleet launched by the British. They would also be in a position to attack the convoys of ships that were taking aid to Russia, and following an attack they could return to port before the Home Fleet could be launched against them. Hitler believed that this role was a much sounder proposition than letting his major units roam the Atlantic sea lanes acting as commerce raiders – that task was best left to the U-boats. He decided that Norway should become the home for the whole of his battlefleet. All of his capital ships were to be brought home to Germany, refitted and then stationed in Norway. It was completely unacceptable to keep the warships in Brest, being bombed day and night by the RAF. Hitler summoned the commander-in-chief of the *Kriegsmarine*, Admiral Erich Raeder, to a meeting and told him the news. As soon as it was practical, he demanded, the battlefleet at Brest was to return to Germany; a breakout into the Atlantic was no longer an option for the vessels.

By the time that autumn arrived, repairs to the three warships were nearing completion. They would all soon be ready for sea once more with their destination no longer to the west into the Atlantic, but to the north-east to Germany. The question was, however, just how would they get there? There were two possible routes: first, northwards towards Iceland, then east and south round the British Isles into the North Sea and, second, there was the more direct route through the English Channel to the German North Sea ports. Both routes were fraught with danger.

The northern route passed close by the Home Fleet anchorage at Scapa Flow. Once the departure of the battlecruisers was spotted, it would be a relatively easy task for the Royal Navy to assemble a powerful force across their path to annihilate them. The other route via the English Channel would take them through the narrow passage of the Dover Straits, bringing the ships to within 20 miles of the English coast, its guns and its airfields. The ships would have to run the gauntlet of a great number of coastal artillery guns, bombers and naval warships, whilst confined to a stretch of sea where manoeuvre was impossible. Both routes seemed suicidal.

Admiral Raeder was appalled with Hitler's views regarding the usefulness of major naval units; he still thought they should use their great strength as commerce raiders in the open Atlantic. He tried to put off returning them to Germany as long as he could. Then events happened that brought the whole question of the effectiveness of capital ships into question. The Japanese launched an aerial attack on the US Pacific Fleet in the naval base at Pearl Harbor in December 1941, damaging and sinking a number of US capital ships. Further disaster struck when the British battlecruiser *Repulse* and the modern battleship *Prince of Wales* were also sunk by Japanese bombers. The events showed how vulnerable these great ships were to air attack. The American battleships lost at Pearl Harbor were all at anchor in a defended port, and the two British warships were in open sea off Malaya. Neither position helped stop their demise. These two incidents changed strategic thinking forever: naval supremacy, wielded through the power of capital ships as the means of dominating world events, had been superseded by air power.

With the USA now having entered the war, its major warships became allied to the British cause in the Atlantic and there was no longer any question of Germany ever sending its major units into the ocean to attack merchantmen. That policy was now dead; the Brest ships would have to return to Germany via one of the two routes that had already been identified.

RAF photo-reconnaissance photograph of the docks at Brest in late 1941. The *Prinz Eugen* and the *Gneisenau* are both in dry dock and the *Scharnhorst* has left port on manoeuvres after repairs. The interpreter at the photo-reconnaissance interpretation section has noted that he has not been fooled by the tanker left tied up along the quay in the berth previously held by the *Scharnhorst* to imitate the battlecruiser. (National Archives Crown Copyright)

Although the decision to return the ships to their home ports was one that was hard to argue with, Admiral Raeder still had great reservations. Neither route, he reasoned, gave any hope of the vessels being able to make it back to Germany intact. Nonetheless, as ordered by Hitler, he issued instructions to Naval Group West in Paris and to Vizeadmiral Otto Ciliax, now in command of the warships at Brest, to consider how they would get the vessels back to Germany. Planners located in France went to work on the problem and discussed every possibility at length. Hitler became annoyed by the delays and pre-empted their decision. He decided that the warships would use the direct route through the English Channel, relying on surprise and overwhelming air cover to see them through. There was no more need for discussion; Hitler told his admirals to get on with it.

On 22 January 1942, Hitler summoned a special meeting to discuss the operation. Raeder pessimistically opened the procedures and immediately handed over to Ciliax to outline to the Führer the plan that had been produced. Ciliax also gave his presentation with a sense of pessimism. 'It was decided,' he explained, 'that the ships would leave Brest under cover of darkness and make the actual passage through the narrowest part of the passage in daylight allowing the maximum air cover to be available at what would be the most critical part of the voyage.' He warned that the volume of fighter cover required to ward off British aircraft was great and anything short of what was needed would lead to certain disaster. Hitler agreed with the plan and promised that the necessary aircraft would be available, although the *Luftwaffe* had their doubts as to whether they could comply with this directive, as their commitment to the Eastern Front was considerable.

Hitler thought the plan would succeed, for he felt sure that his opponents would not be able to react quickly enough to stop the ships. He explained his reasons to this gathering of senior commanders: 'In view of past experience,' he said, 'I do not believe the British are capable of making and carrying out lightning decisions. I do not believe that they will be as swift as the naval staff and Vizeadmiral Ciliax assume in transferring their bomber and fighter aircraft to the south-eastern part of England for an attack on our ships in the Dover Straits.' He then went on to explain why he would insist on the operation going ahead. He reasoned that the ships in Brest would inevitably be destroyed by continual bombing if they stayed where they were. 'The situation of the Brest Group is like a patient with cancer who is doomed unless he submits to an operation. An operation, on the other hand, even though it may have to be drastic, will at least offer some hope that the patient's life may yet be saved. It must therefore be attempted.'

Meanwhile, the main concern worrying the British regarding the three warships holed up in Brest remained the threat they posed to shipping in the Atlantic. Although aerial reconnaissance had shown that the ships were damaged, there was no certain way of knowing the exact nature of the damage or how the repairs were progressing. Whilst the ships were in port the situation was clear, but if their berths suddenly became empty who knew where they could disappear to? The matter had been the cause of great apprehension ever since they had arrived in the port.

Both the Admiralty and the RAF had given thought to the problem. The Royal Navy knew that they could not blockade the port, for any of its vessels patrolling close to the French coast would attract the attentions of the *Luftwaffe* aircraft stationed in the region. Its main hope rested on the early detection of any German movements allowing time for a strike force to be organized against the ships and this surveillance was best left to the aircraft of the RAF. The Admiralty and RAF high command had also considered that the enemy battlefleet might realize that to remain in Brest under continuous aerial bombardment was bound to end in disaster, and they could decide to risk the consequences of making a dash for German ports via the English Channel. They also concluded that should this happen the ships would choose to pass through the Dover Straits at night. This would mean that a good part of the voyage from Brest would have to be made in daylight and could easily be spotted by vigilant air patrols. Steps to detect the enemy fleet in case it chose to use the Channel route were increased throughout the remainder of 1941. By 1942, after the early Allied maritime disasters in the Pacific, it became increasingly clear that the Germans would never risk their battlecruisers in the North Atlantic again. They had to use the Channel route.

PLANNING AND TRAINING

Repairs to the *Scharnhorst*, *Gneisenau* and *Prinz Eugen* continued through 1941, in spite of regular bombing raids by the RAF. By December aerial reconnaissance showed that the three warships in Brest appeared to be seaworthy, and information from a variety of sources, including the French Resistance, indicated that they were preparing to leave port.

At Naval Group West's headquarters in Paris and in Brest, the German planners who were working on the breakout laboured in complete secrecy. Very few people were party to any details of the forthcoming operation, or that it would take place at all. By early 1942, a strategy that the German commanders thought might just be able to get the ships back home had been devised and approved. For it to work, three main problems had to be overcome: first, enough fighter aircraft had to be assembled along the route to provide a continuous air umbrella over the ships once daylight came; second, a safe path had to be swept through the numerous minefields that littered the Channel; and finally, the British radar that monitored the Channel passage had to be jammed in such a way that it became blind. Of course, there were many more obstacles than these to be dealt with, but without these three main problems being solved the operation would inevitably end in disaster.

Responsibility for providing air cover for the breakout was vested in Oberst Adolf Galland, one of the *Luftwaffe*'s most famous fighter aces. Galland was a much-decorated veteran, renowned for his exploits with the Condor Legion in Spain and in aerial dogfights over France and Britain in 1940. He had been given approval by the *Führer* to assemble the necessary number of aircraft for what was titled Operation *Cerberus*. It was not an easy task to gather the quantity of aircraft required, for he met resistance from senior officers within *Luftwaffe* headquarters. Relations with the *Kriegsmarine* became a little strained when the air force was asked to provide a great number of aircraft for what was a purely naval operation. Its commitments on the Eastern Front had meant that it was already short of aircraft in the West. Galland was grudgingly allocated three fighter groups

Oberst Adolf Galland, perhaps the most famous of all German fighter pilots who took part in the Battle of Britain. During Operation *Cerberus*, Galland had been given approval by Hitler to assemble the number of fighters he thought necessary to protect the German battlefleet during their dash along the English Channel, even though the war against Russia was at that time making extraordinary demands on every available aircraft. (IWM HU 59697)

and 30 night-fighters for the operation, which amounted to around 280 aircraft. These were to be stationed on airfields close to the Channel so as to be able to provide continuous sorties over the warships throughout the whole of the critical part of the passage.

The plan called for the night-fighters to cover the period before dawn as the battlefleet rounded the Channel Islands and moved into the English Channel proper. Then the day-fighters would take over, organized in such a way that 16 aircraft would be flying close air patrols over the ships at any one time. Galland would have his headquarters at Le Touquet, half way along the Channel, with command posts at Caen for the early part of the route and Schipol in Holland for the last leg of the voyage. On board the *Scharnhorst*, Oberst Max Ibel would command the main seaborne fighter command centre with operational fighter controllers also placed on both of the other two main warships. Galland's headquarters would organize the timing of the air umbrella, whilst Ibel would have the responsibility for coordinating the aircraft once they were over the ships through direct radio-telephone links to the fighters. To achieve some proficiency in this type of aerial activity, all of the aircrews involved flew training sorties to test their equipment and improve their ability to intercept and protect ships at sea without knowing the nature of the operation that was ahead of them.

At this point in the war, the English Channel was full of mines. Both sides guarded the approaches to their ports with large minefields and both also covered whole strips of the seaway with mined areas in order to force enemy ships away from certain sectors of the Channel. Spurious mine-laying was also carried out by aircraft dropping mines along known routes used by the other side. One day a passage might be free of hazards only to find that the next day a ship would be sunk by a recently laid mine dropped from an aircraft, or placed by a swift moving mine-laying vessel. The work of minesweepers on both sides was relentless.

Kommodore Friedrich Ruge was in command of all German minesweeping activities along the Channel coast, and Naval Group West now ordered him to ensure that a lane was cleared through the Channel for the battlefleet. He was to do this in complete secrecy. Ruge took just two of his planners into his confidence and devised a method that kept the task from everyone else involved. The preferred route through the Channel was divided up into sections and small areas. His flotilla captains were then given the task of sweeping a carefully defined zone without reference to any other. Ruge's aide then plotted the clearance of each of these sectors until a whole mine-free lane had been swept. These activities were only to be carried out at night, and several explanations were given to the seamen involved to allay suspicions. To the crews involved, there seemed to be little logic in the tasks they had been given. This work continued as planned right up until the time of the breakout, even though the weather was sometimes wild and wintry.

The third of the main foreseeable problems was the question of British coastal radar. It was clear to the Germans that their enemy had an effective system in place by the number of times their convoys and individual ships had been attacked without prior warning. They knew the British were watching the Channel from a string of radar stations located along the south coast of England and they knew how effective this radar could be. It had to be silenced whilst the battle fleet was in passage.

The head of the *Luftwaffe* Signals Service was General der Luftnachrichtentruppe Wolfgang Martini, who was given the task of silencing the British coastal radar. Martini's experts had much earlier identified the wavelengths of the British equipment and had already constructed a number of transmitting stations along the coast of northern France capable of jamming it. Martini now devised a plan that would gradually reduce the effectiveness of the enemy's radar without alerting its controllers to events in the Channel. If the jamming was just switched on as the battlefleet approached, the British would know that something important was happening. Martini had to be more

Swordfish and Beaufort torpedo aircraft dispersed on an airfield along the south coast, most likely at Lee-on-Solent. Depth charges on trolleys remain close by, ready to be loaded onto the aircraft for an anti-submarine mission. (IWM CH 635)

subtle than that. He proposed that at the start of each day in the weeks preceding the breakout, his teams would transmit signals set to the same frequencies as the British to mask the reflections of the radar beams and to simulate interference. As daylight began these regular bouts of 'interference' would increasingly be accepted by the British operators as a natural atmospheric phenomenon. Martini's teams would then gradually lengthen the times of their transmissions day by day until long periods of jamming were achieved without raising British alarm.

The secret activities involved in dealing with these problems were just some of the tasks required by Naval Group West to organize the breakout. Also needed was some protection for the battlefleet down at sea level. Ciliax did not know exactly what the British would send against him as his ships made their way up the Channel. Certainly there would be torpedo-firing aircraft, fighters and bombers, but what naval vessels would sally out from their ports to meet him? Destroyers and torpedo boats would be sure to be encountered and possibly capital ships of the Home Fleet if they were alerted in time. The larger vessels would be handled by his heavy unit's large guns, but Ciliax also needed close naval protection from smaller German craft, and arrangements were made to divert some of these ships to Brest to join the battlefleet.

First to be allocated to protect the heavy units were the destroyers. The flotilla assigned to the task, 5th Destroyer Flotilla, was now directed to Brest to join the major units. Commanding these warships was Kapitän zur

See Erich Bey, who flew his flag in destroyer *Z.29*. His flotilla consisted of the destroyers *Richard Beitzen*, *Paul Jacobi*, *Frederich Ihn*, *Hermann Schoemann*, *Z.25* and *Z.29*. All of these warships were modern vessels; the first four of the destroyers named here were built between 1935 and 1937, just a few years before the outbreak of war, whilst *Z.25* and *Z.29* were only two years old at the start of the operation. A seventh ship had been allocated for the breakout, but this destroyer, the *Bruno Heinmann*, was sunk on 25 January whilst passing through the Channel towards Brest. It had the misfortune of hitting a mine that had been newly laid by the minelayer HMS *Plover* between 15 and 23 January.

Three flotillas of fast E-Boats were also allocated to the operation. The 2nd, 3rd and 5th Torpedo Boat Flotillas would, in turn, meet the capital ships as they passed the sea areas off Cherbourg, Le Havre and Cap Gris Nez to provide a close screen around the battlefleet as it sailed through the crucial part of the route.

The most vulnerable section of the passage would be through the narrow Straits of Dover (Pas de Calais). The 21 miles separating England and France at this point would not allow any intricate manoeuvring by the formation in order to escape the fire of the coastal batteries lining the English coast, nor attack by fast inshore craft. The German warships would have to pass directly through the gap at high speed and hope to evade the worst that the British could throw at them. To help hold down the fire of the heavy-calibre British coastal guns, German long-range batteries around the Pas de Calais would lay down counter-battery fire to force the British gunners to keep their heads down.

To the British, the possibility of a German dash through the Channel had been under consideration for the previous nine months, and an operation code named *Fuller* had been devised to deal with such an eventuality. The plan did not, however, call for a terribly impressive gathering of forces. The British effort mainly relied on light naval forces and attack from the air to halt the enemy passage. Even though the major warships of the Home Fleet were available in the north of Scotland, they were not to be used.

The Admiralty was insistent that should an enemy breakout through the Channel occur, none of its capital warships would be sent against the German battlefleet. The risk to the ships from the *Luftwaffe* was deemed to be too great. The First Sea Lord, Admiral Sir Dudley Pound, had decreed that his major units would be vulnerable to air attack if they ventured too close to the enemy-held coastline of France and the Low Countries. The fear of further losses of capital ships so soon after the sinking of the *Hood*, *Repulse* and *Prince of Wales* made the Royal Navy shrink from the task. On the one hand, such a position was understandable – the loss of any capital ship would be a blow to Britain's maritime prestige – but on the other hand the destruction of this group of enemy vessels would at a stroke reduce Germany's major fleet to just one battleship, the *Tirpitz*, and six heavy cruisers. Set against the combined battlefleets of the Royal Navy and the US Navy, such puny opposition would be relatively easy to contain in northern waters. Contrast that with the possibility of the *Scharnhorst*,

Two of the German destroyers screen close-by the *Prinz Eugen* during the early part of the Channel Dash. Their abstract-shaped dazzle camouflage looks particularly bold from such a close viewpoint. (IWM MH4972)

Gneisenau and the *Prinz Eugen* joining up with the *Tirpitz* to form probably the most powerful modern battlefleet of the war and the risk might have been worth taking. After all, the Germans were risking their ships in a constricted seaway, close to an enemy coast with powerful numbers of enemy aircraft and fast torpedo craft ranged against them, so why not commit the Royal Navy as well?

If the Home Fleet had contemplated intercepting the enemy ships, the action would have to take place in the sea area off the West Frisian Islands on the north Dutch coast. The distance from Brest to this area is around 575 miles, whilst it was only 450 miles from Scapa Flow. Given early warning of the departure of the German ships from the French port, the Home Fleet could be in position and waiting to attack the German fleet as it reached the area. Such an attack would have been after the enemy ships had already sailed through the Channel and after they had run the gauntlet of torpedo-bombers, motor torpedo craft, heavy bombers, fighters, destroyers and mines, and after the *Luftwaffe* planes and their pilots had been in constant action against the RAF and were tired. The enemy fleet by then could have been slowed down or even crippled to such an extent that it would be at the mercy of the mighty ships of Home Fleet.

Battleships were built for the purpose of engaging the enemy's capital ships. During World War II, Allied capital ships actually spent most of their time escorting convoys and taking part in shore bombardments during amphibious landings, whilst the German big ships acted as commerce raiders.

There were few actual ship-vs.-ship engagements. In fact, no battleship was sunk by conventional bombers whilst underway at sea during the war, for it was near impossible for bombers to hit a warship moving at 30 knots that was taking evasive action. The most potent weapons pitted against capital ships were torpedoes from torpedo-bombers and bombs from dive-bombers, as was shown in the sinking of the *Repulse* and *Prince of Wales* by the Japanese. Germany had, in early 1942, just one main torpedo-bomber in service, the obsolete Heinkel He 115 floatplane, whilst its main dive-bomber was the also-obsolete short-range Junkers Ju 87 Stuka, most of which were then in service on the Eastern Front. The threat to Dudley Pound's Home Fleet from the few operational German torpedo-bombers and dive-bombers that were available in Holland was probably not sufficient an excuse to prevent its use against such important targets. It was also expected that the enemy would pass through the Dover Straits in darkness, another reason why the German bomber threat would have been less successful than imagined by the Admiralty. But the decision had been made; the Home Fleet would not come south to tackle the enemy ships.

The absence of heavy units to oppose the breakout resulted in many smaller craft being committed to Operation *Fuller*. The final naval plan for combating the 'Channel Dash' by the enemy, should it occur, was based on the notion that the German ships would pass through the narrowest part of the voyage in darkness. Ever since the German ships had arrived in Brest, the British had assumed that if they chose to return to Germany via the shortest route, the passage through the Dover Straits would be in the hours just before dawn. Such a move would enable them to use the cover of darkness to help conceal their progress up the English Channel into the North Sea during the most critical period of the whole voyage. The plan for Operation *Fuller* was therefore completely formulated on this assumption.

For the ships to arrive off the Pas de Calais coast in complete darkness, they would have to leave Brest in daylight. The British were confident that such a move would be easily spotted by standing air and sea patrols and would therefore give an adequate warning period to galvanize all of the forces required for Operation *Fuller*. However, in winter with its shorter periods of daylight, if they left Brest just before dusk, they could possibly make the 350-mile dash through the night to arrive in the Straits of Dover just before dawn. This was thought to be the German's most likely option.

The closest observation kept on the port of Brest was made by submarines. This was a most hazardous task, for the sea off the French port was lively with German shipping. Late in 1941, the Admiralty realized that the enemy ships were close to being ready to sail and decided to increase the watch made on the port. It ordered a total of seven submarines to take up patrol lines off Brest in the Bay of Biscay from 24 December to provide an 'iron ring' around the port. The craft were all old training submarines, some of World War I vintage, normally in use for working-up new crews and exercising with anti-submarine vessels. They were slow and their engines were noisy even when submerged, and they were therefore unable to operate too close to the enemy-held shore for fear of detection. It was a bold move to station such a pack of

submarines off Brest, but one that proved to be unsustainable, for the withdrawal of this large number of submarines from home waters necessitated the stopping of all submariner training. On 2 January 1942, the patrols were called off and the submarine watch reverted to just two vessels.

Daylight reconnaissance flights could determine, cloud cover permitting, whether or not the enemy ships were still at their berths. If they slipped away in darkness and disappeared into the night, then other methods of tracking them had to be used. The next line of reconnaissance was provided by RAF Coastal Command and was organized to cover this eventuality. If the ships moved towards the Channel they would be detected by one of three overlapping standing dusk to dawn patrols that were carried out each night by Hudson aircraft.

The first of these patrols was called 'Stopper' and covered the coastline from Brest to Ushant. The second patrol, 'Line South East', monitored the sea area Ushant to the Île-de-Bréhat off the Brittany coast. The third of these monitoring flights, 'Habo', patrolled along a line from Le Havre to Boulogne. The Hudson aircraft of Coastal Command carrying out the flights were equipped with Anti-Surface Vessel (ASV) Mark II radar capable of locating ships at ranges of up to 30 miles. The nature of the patrols was such that if one of the flights missed the ships, the others would be sure to spot them.

When daylight came, RAF Fighter Command would take over the watch. Its patrols operated under the codeword 'Jim Crow'. At dawn each day, a 'Jim Crow' Spitfire took off to scan the Channel eastwards from Cap Gris Nez to Flushing, whilst another fighter aircraft flew in the opposite direction to search westwards from Cap Griz Nez to Le Havre. They were seeking likely targets for further operations later in the day by cannon-firing fighters and Hurricane bombers. Naval HQ at Dover would also be informed of any enemy shipping in case they wished to dispatch motor torpedo boats (MTBs) to intercept them. The patrols were not specifically part of Operation *Fuller*, they were just routine sorties flown by 91 Squadron from Hawkinge airfield in Kent. As such their pilots had no idea that a watch was being kept for the German battlefleet. It was another example of the pointless secrecy that surrounded *Fuller*.

Also watching the Germans' planned route were a number of British radar stations sited along the coast, all of which were using equipment with a much longer range than that carried by the Coastal Command aircraft. These stations could pick up enemy coastal traffic 80 miles away moving along the Channel between the French ports.

With the five standing air patrols and the coastal radar stations covering the only route through the Channel, the planners of Operation *Fuller* were confident that the enemy ships would be easily detected, even in darkness or bad weather. Once the German warships had been spotted, the offensive phase of *Fuller* would be put into action. All of the services would combine to make the enemy's passage through the straits a hazardous one. First into action would be the MTBs located at Dover and Ramsgate. These would be supported by motor gun boats (MGBs) and could launch their torpedoes at the enemy fleet at ranges around 4,000yds. Next to attack would be the painfully slow-moving, but very effective, Swordfish torpedo aircraft of the Fleet Air Arm, which had performed so well against the battleship *Bismarck* the previous year. The Swordfish provided a stable platform from which to release torpedoes, but the flimsy biplanes were vulnerable to fighter aircraft and could only really be used effectively at night. They required a good fighter escort with them to fend off the enemy whilst they made their run in to their targets. Coastal Command's Beaufort torpedo aircraft would attack next.

Following that, the Army's large-calibre coastal artillery guarding the Dover Straits would open up on the enemy when the ships came into range. By this time, Bomber Command would also have squadrons of aircraft in the air, lining up to attack the German battlefleet east of the Dover Straits. It was hoped that by then at least one of the enemy major units would have been hit and slowed down sufficiently to enable it to be dispatched finally by the bombers. As the enemy moved away from the English Channel, six destroyers from Harwich would attack with torpedoes. Ahead of the fleeing ships, the RAF would lay mines in their path and launch yet more bombing attacks. By this time the German fleet would either be sunk or badly damaged. It was disappointing that the Admiralty had decided that the Home Fleet could not take advantage of such a prospect to attack then with its heavy units.

Bomber Command had planned to have a bomber force of around 100 aircraft available for Operation *Fuller*, standing at four hours notice; this was around one-third of its effective strength. At this time in the war, with a number of squadrons out of the line for re-equipping and re-arming, Bomber Command could muster around 300 aircraft each day for

Beaufort torpedo-bomber of RAF 86 Squadron. The Beaufort was developed from the Bristol Blenheim bomber and was introduced into service with RAF Coastal Command in January 1940.
(IWM CH 7945)

operations. Twenty aircraft from each of its five groups were allocated to *Fuller* and kept at four hours readiness. Of the other 200 bombers, half would be committed to normal bombing operations whilst the other half was preparing for the next day's missions. The *Fuller* aircraft were rotated within each group so that different crews would be allocated for different days. Of these 100 aircraft, if circumstances permitted, 20–25 of them would be allocated to attack the docks at Brest.

Fighter Command's main mission was to protect the bomber and torpedo-bomber attacks on the ships. Fortunately it had many bases along the south coast close to the Channel. No. 11 Group covered London and the south east, a region that included the sea area in which the enemy would likely be attacked. It had 13 Spitfire and three Hurricane squadrons available for the battle. Other aircraft from adjacent groups could also be vectored into the attack, with No. 10 Group's fighters covering the south-west of England and No. 12 Group protecting the East Anglia region.

That was the plan for Operation *Fuller*. On paper it looked good, but there were inherent problems that would lessen its impact. Its intention was to overwhelm the enemy by successive and continual attacks all through the Channel, and it relied on coordinated efforts being made by Coastal Command, the Royal Navy and the RAF. Such close cooperation was, at that time in the war, difficult to put into practice. All services had liaison officers in the various control centres to coordinate actions, but all used separate communication systems that excluded the others. In the heat of the action, not everyone might be informed of everyone else's intentions and actions.

THE CHANNEL DASH

On 4 January 1942, the Admiralty published an appreciation which indicated that *Scharnhorst* and *Prinz Eugen* could sail from Brest any time after 24 January. *Gneisenau* would take longer and would most likely not be ready until early February. It also suggested that although some working-up practices had been carried out, it was not considered that the ships were fully efficient. The signal went on: 'There are no indications of the intentions of the enemy. A breakout to Germany or Trondjheim by the ships at Brest aided by *Tirpitz*, or some other concerted action by all three heavy units, seems to be the most probable course, but a dash to an Italian port in the Mediterranean can not be disregarded.'

It was becoming more likely that the German ships would soon be ready to set sail from Brest. As the above signal indicates, whilst the general opinion was that they would attempt a dash through the Channel, other options were still available to them for which the Admiralty had to take steps to counter. If they went south for the Mediterranean or pushed west into the Atlantic, Force 'H' at Gibraltar would sally out to meet them. The Americans were also asked to make ready their plans should the German ships become loose in the Atlantic.

On 30 January, the carrier *Eagle* in the Clyde was put on four hours notice to be ready should the battlecruisers break out into the Atlantic. The Admiralty were also concerned about the security of a large troop convoy that was due to leave the UK for Sierra Leone on 14 February. Escort for the convoy was to be provided by the battleship *Malaya*, the cruiser *Hermione* and several destroyers. The battleship *Rodney* was now ordered north from Gibraltar to give added protection.

As each day's reconnaissance reports were received, it became clear that the time was approaching when the battlefleet would be ready to sail. After the 'iron ring' of submarines had been withdrawn from the sea area off Brest in early January, just two vessels continued to keep watch on the French port. A third submarine, the relatively modern *Sealion*, was also sent to patrol the area off Brest on 5 February, but its task was mainly to monitor any breakout to the south-west.

11 FEBRUARY 1942

**2125hrs
The ships leave the harbour at Brest**

Vice-Admiral Bertram Ramsay, Commander-in-Chief Dover, who coordinated the main response to Operation *Fuller*, the climax of which took place in the Dover Straits just 15 miles from his headquarters in Dover Castle. (IWM A23442)

Admiral Sir Max Horton, Admiral Commanding Submarines, had been told by the Admiralty that his brief was to watch for the enemy ships attempting to sail into the Atlantic or south to the Mediterranean. The route north-east to the English Channel was to be monitored by surface craft and Coastal Command's aircraft. Two of Horton's submarines, *H43* and *H50*, were in his words 'out-of-date and noisy', and were ordered to keep station along the 100 fathoms line some 80 miles from the French port to the south. Their watch was to spot the enemy formation if it moved towards the Mediterranean. The captain of the *Sealion*, Lieutenant-Commander G.R. Colvin, had been told to patrol closer in to Brest and position himself during the hours of daylight near to the swept lane that the enemy ships would sail through if they came out on exercise. If circumstances permitted, Colvin was at liberty to attack the German heavy units, but all concerned knew that any such sortie made by the Germans was sure to be covered by the protection of numerous anti-submarine vessels and the *Sealion* would be lucky to escape any such attack.

On 3 February a signal was sent to HQ Coastal Command and Vice-Admiral Dover, initiating a move of the only Swordfish torpedo-bombers that were available for Operation *Fuller*. 'All six aircraft of 825 Squadron now at Lee on Solent are now required to move to Manston as soon as weather permits', stated the signal. 'The Squadron Commander is to operate only those crews which he considers would contribute to the achievement of the object.' The phrasing of the signal acknowledged that 825 Squadron had been reformed only two months previously and some of its crews were well short of the training necessary to bring them up to operational readiness.

The Warships Depart

At noon on 11 February, Vizeadmiral Ciliax called a conference of senior officers on board his flagship the *Scharnhorst*. At the meeting he told his captains, Kapitän zur See Kurt Hoffmann of the *Scharnhorst*, Kapitän zur See Otto Fein of the *Gneisenau* and Kapitän zur See Helmuth Brinkmann of the *Prinz Eugen*, that both weather and tides were favourable that night for the start of Operation *Cerberus*. Escort ships were in place, fighter cover had been assembled and minefields had been cleared. His ships would leave harbour at 1930hrs under the guise of departing on a night exercise. Their crews were not to be told that the battlefleet was bound for their homeland through the English Channel.

Not far away, lying still at periscope depth 6 miles from the mouth of Brest harbour, Commander Colvin kept the submarine *Sealion* on station as he watched various small craft plying their way in and out of the French port. He spotted no major ship movements. At 1400hrs, his vessel slipped away on the ebb tide to retire to a point 30 miles from shore, where it would surface and charge its batteries, safe in the knowledge that the enemy heavy units were still tied up in port. *H43* and *H50* remained on their watch 40 more miles away to the south. This first line of detection was now out of sight of the port of Brest.

At 1827hrs, a Hudson aircraft of 224 Squadron piloted by Pilot Officer Wilson took off to begin the first of the 'Stopper' patrols, keeping watch on the waters in the vicinity of Brest. Wilson had been ordered to fly a north–south patrol line to the west of the port, looking for enemy shipping movements. At no time was Wilson or his crew briefed to be on the look out for a possible enemy battlefleet containing capital ships. The mission was completely routine and had been flown since the previous September when the squadron had arrived at St Eval. The aircraft was equipped with air-to-ship radar with forward facing aerials that were capable of detecting surface vessels and other aircraft up to 30 miles ahead of him.

When Wilson's Hudson was just over half way to the patrol area, at 1915hrs, the wireless operator reported a blip 7 miles to starboard on the ASV radar set. Wilson banked away to the west to investigate, and two minutes later an enemy Ju 88 aircraft flashed across his path slightly above him. The German fighter-bomber was clearly visible in silhouette.

Wilson immediately began taking evasive action and ordered the wireless operator to switch off the radio and the ASV radar. When asked later why he did this, Wilson replied that the sets gave off a certain amount of light and he wished everything to remain as black as possible to avoid detection by the enemy aircraft. As soon as he was sure that he had shaken off the German intruder and the danger had passed, Wilson gave instructions for the radar to be switched on again. The operator complied, but found that the set was not working. All power had been lost and the set appeared dead. The wireless operator tried the main fuse but, in the darkness, felt that it was still intact and OK. With visibility outside near to zero, where even the sea below them was invisible, Wilson ordered a signal to be sent advising control that he was returning to base. Wireless reception was poor and the control at St Eval did not know that the Hudson was pulling out of the patrol until just ten minutes before the aircraft landed. The fault was proved to be a blown fuse.

At 1930hrs, just as Wilson's Hudson was withdrawing from its intended watch over the waters off Brest, the ships of Ciliax's battlefleet were casting off from their moorings to begin their epic journey home. At that same moment, air raid sirens began to wail, signalling the start of another bombing raid on the port by the RAF. One by one the searchlights around the town burst into life, probing the night sky with bright streaks of light. Then the familiar sound of anti-aircraft fire reverberated off the hills close by as the first of the night's bombers droned overhead. Soon the night sky was criss-crossed by tracer fire and further illuminated with the bright flashes of bombs

**11 FEBRUARY
1942**

**2350hrs
The ships pass
to the north of
Ushant**

as they detonated. Then, gradually, the whole of the port area was smothered by a suffocating blanket as smoke generators poured out artificial fog to cover the ships. Ciliax gave the order to halt the sailings and sat impotently inside his ship as the Wellington bombers came over one by one to drop their bombs. When the last of the bombers had left, a photo-reconnaissance aircraft swept over the port recording the damage and getting a fix on the heavy warships, which remained stationary alongside their berths. When the photographs were later developed, RAF intelligence was pleased to report that the German battlecruisers had not sailed that day.

Eventually, after some 90 minutes, the bombers left and the all-clear sounded. Vizeadmiral Ciliax then sent a signal to his ships for them to cast off once again. One by one the heavy units of the battlefleet were pulled clear of their berths and swung around by tugs to head for the harbour entrance, feeling their way slowly through the steadily dispersing artificial fog that still hung over the inner part of the port. After edging their way clear of the breakwater, the attendant destroyers moved into formation alongside the three large warships and the small fleet moved out into the open sea. *Scharnhorst* led the way, followed by *Gneisenau* and *Prinz Eugen* in line astern. It was 2130hrs; the breakout had begun.

Over the Channel at St Eval in England, Pilot Officer Wilson had landed his aircraft and taxied to the airfield's dispersal point. 'I was met by a man from the Operations Room telling me to take my crew to aircraft "K" which was in "A" Flight on the other side of the aerodrome and get off the ground

Two of the heavy German warships, and an attendant destroyer, make their way up the English Channel through a gradually worsening sea during Operation *Cerberus*. (IWM MH5007)

again as soon as we could. At the same time I was told that the Flying Control wanted to speak to me.' Wilson sent his crew over to the spare Hudson and was taken by van to see the flight controller. He was told to take his new aircraft back to the 'Stopper' patrol line and remain on station until 2340hrs.

When Wilson joined his crew in aircraft 'K' they were already running up its engines, but they were still both quite cold. Although the aircraft was on standby for any eventuality, its engines had not been started since its previous flight. It took some time to get the Hudson ready, as Wilson later explained.

> We had to wait ten or fifteen minutes for the starboard engine's oil temperature to reach 50°C for running it up, and then it would only reach 2,500 revolutions at full boost instead of 2,700. Also the port engine was dropping 150 revolutions on one magneto and so it was another quarter of an hour before I could get the cylinder heads hot enough to dry up the plug and get it satisfactory. Eventually we got it right and we taxied out and took off at 21.35 hours.

It was not until 2238hrs that Wilson was able to resume his patrol off Brest. In the meantime, the enemy battlefleet had departed. A blown fuse and a damp plug had allowed Vizeadmiral Ciliax and his ships to evade the British second line of detection.

Fifteen minutes before Wilson's 'Stopper' flight had reached the area of its patrol, the second 'Stopper' Hudson, piloted by Squadron Leader Bartlett, took off from St Eval to fly the relief patrol for the first 'Stopper'. Wilson continued to fly a dog-leg course off Brest until his mission was completed as instructed at 2343hrs and then returned to base. The task was then given over to Bartlett's aircraft for the remainder of the night hours. Neither of the ASV operators in these aircraft saw anything unusual enough to report, even though both aircraft passed over, or close to, the route of the escaping German ships and the operators could see the shape of the coastline on their radar sets.

At 1845hrs, not long after the first 'Stopper' patrol had taken off from St Eval earlier that evening, a second Hudson left the ground. This aircraft, piloted by Sergeant A. Wilson, was to fly the 'Line South East' patrol, sweeping the sea lanes from Ushant to the Bay of the Seine. Wilson arrived at his patrol line at 1936hrs, just as the German warships were first preparing to sail. Minutes after starting to fly the prescribed patrol line, it soon became clear that the aircraft's radar was not working. The ASV operator, Sergeant Barber, thought he should be getting an echo from the isle of Ushant, but nothing appeared on his screen. The aircraft continued its patrol along the fixed SE Line as Barber tried to re-tune the set. Another search was tried without getting any results from the sea below. It was clear that the ASV set had broken down. After reporting the failure to the control, a message was received at 2139hrs ordering the Hudson to return to base. At that moment, 50 miles away to the south, the German warships were negotiating their way out of Brest. When the aircraft returned, its radar set was examined. Nothing was found to be wrong with the instrument. It was later returned to service and worked completely satisfactorily.

12 FEBRUARY
1942

0125hrs
The ships enter
the English
Channel

At around midnight, Ciliax's line of ships were off Ushant. They had been cruising at 27 knots and had started to make up the time lost during the air raid on Brest. As it rounded the Breton island, the battlefleet altered course to starboard to enter the English Channel. At 0125hrs the ships swung to the north-east, making a line that would bring them just to the north of the German-occupied Channel Islands. Here was the first crucial moment of the voyage, for it was the point of no return. Once into the Channel there was no going back. The secret was now out – all those on board the great warships were told that their destination was Germany; they were going home.

Further along the Channel, the first 'Habo' patrol flown by a Hudson of 223 Squadron had taken off from Thorney Island near Portsmouth at 0037hrs. The aircraft flew to a point just off the French coast near Le Havre, arriving at the start point of its patrol at 0112hrs. Its pilot, Flight Sergeant Smith, flew the line of his patrol almost to Cherbourg, then turned and flew east again, keeping within 12 miles of the French coast. Smith's patrol involved flying two circuits of this course. His ASV operator saw nothing all night but three friendly motor launches. The enemy ships were still off the coast of Brittany by the time Smith reached the end of his patrol at 0335hrs and returned to base.

The second 'Habo' patrol began when Flying Officer Alexander brought his Hudson into position at 0430hrs. His patrol took him across the Bay of the Seine westwards as far as Cherbourg, flying a triangular route to cover both the inner bay and the outer line through the Channel. Like that flown by Flight Sergeant Smith, it lasted around two hours and consisted of two circuits. Both of these 'Habo' flights were told the routes and timings of their patrols, and when they were finished they were to return to base.

Alexander landed his aircraft back at base at 0715hrs still in darkness; he was scheduled to return at 0725hrs. Nothing had been seen on the ASV radar during the whole of the mission, save for the outline of the French coast. As Alexander touched his aircraft down in the gathering fog that was rolling across the airfield, the German fleet was off Cherbourg in the very area that he had been patrolling just an hour earlier. There was later some suggestion that Alexander's patrol was recalled early due to the possibility of fog closing in over Thorney Island and that if he had continued flying his mission he might have spotted the enemy. He insisted that this was not the case and that he had flown the whole of his mission as ordered before he returned, just two circuits of the prescribed route.

The first light of dawn began at around 0745hrs, but it was almost another hour before it was full daylight. On board *Scharnhorst* action stations had been sounded and all hands went to their battle positions. On the admiral's bridge, Oberst Ibel joined Vizeadmiral Ciliax and made contact with his two controllers on the other heavy ships by signal lamp, making sure that everyone was ready to liaise with Adolf Galland's fighters. At 0750hrs the first of these aircraft came roaring in from astern, firing recognition flares to herald their arrival. The fighters swept over the warships, dipping their wings in salute before climbing up to their operational altitude. Once aloft they began flying in a continuous circular pattern, with their pilots stealing themselves for their

The *Gneisenau* and *Prinz Eugen*, seen from the *Scharnhorst*. Daylight has broken and a careful watch is kept on the sky all around – the crews are ready for the expected appearance of the RAF. (IWM HU35743)

long vigil over the battlefleet. On board the fast-moving ships, the gathering light seemed to expose the vulnerability that their crews felt, each of them knowing that the whole strength of the Royal Navy and the RAF could be gathering just over the horizon, ready for the fateful showdown. Nothing could be further from the truth, for the British were still utterly ignorant of the presence of the battlefleet in the Channel and would remain so for several more hours to come.

The German Ships are Out!

At 0835hrs, with no sightings made of the enemy ships and the critical 'before dawn' hours now past, Vice-Admiral Bertram Ramsay sent a signal from his Dover headquarters indicating that the high-alert status was ended and that all units could revert to four hours notice of readiness. To the British mind, the German heavy units had not tried to force a passage through the Straits of Dover in darkness. The threat was over, until at least the following night.

Out in the Channel to the south-west, Ciliax was being warned of a new minefield that had been laid by the Royal Navy during the night. Naval Command West in Paris had warned the admiral that these mines lay across the path of the battlefleet, and although minesweepers were at work trying to clear a way through the obstacles, they might not be finished before the heavy units arrived in the area. Ciliax knew that to stop would be fatal for his ships and to make a detour round the minefield would be hazardous and time consuming. He decided to trust his luck and ordered

12 FEBRUARY 1942

0830hrs The ships pass through British minefield off Le Havre

Group Captain Victor Beamish, who during his career was awarded the Distinguish Service Order (DSO) and Bar, Distinguished Flying Cross (DFC) and Air Force Cross (AFC). Seen here with the rank of squadron leader, Beamish provided the first definite information that the German ships had left Brest and were in the Channel. Beamish had earned a great reputation during the Battle of Britain as a leading fighter pilot. He was killed in action just six weeks after the Channel Dash. (IWM CH491)

his fleet of ships to steam steadfastly across it, although at a slightly reduced speed. Fortune remained with the admiral – all went well during the crossing and by 0830hrs the German ships were through the danger and had resumed their speed of 27 knots.

At 0845 hours, two Spitfires took off to fly a 'Jim Crow' mission, one covering the Channel north-eastwards from Cap Gris Nez to Flushing, the other flying south-westwards from Cap Gris Nez to Le Havre. The northerly Spitfire saw nothing more than a few fishing boats off Zeebrugge. The other aircraft spotted a number of E-boats leaving Boulogne, heading down Channel towards Dieppe. It continued to the mouth of the River Somme and, at 0904hrs, turned for home. Neither of the fighter pilots saw anything else that struck them as being unusual and returned to base to make their reports. The pilot of the southerly flight had in fact seen the escort E-boats that were to help shepherd the enemy heavy units through the Dover Straits, and if he had continued just a little further to the west would have spotted the German fleet steaming up Channel.

A while earlier, at 0800hrs, Corporal Jones started his shift in charge of the Range and Direction Finding (RDF) station at Beachy Head. Manning the radar screen was Aircraftman Gubbins. At 0824hrs Gubbins reported to Jones that a number of enemy aircraft were off the French coast. 'They were mostly circling around and we reported them to Fighter Command's Filter Room via Pevensey', recalled Jones. 'The aircraft did not seem to be moving much, they just kept circling around.' At 0920hrs Adams had taken over the radar watch and reported that interference had cropped up making the plots difficult to see. 'Just before ten o'clock,' remembers Jones, 'Adams remarked that there was something in the middle of the aircraft which looked like shipping. I took a look myself and came to the conclusion that there were about six vessels with the aircraft. At 1014 and 1016 hours two more plots were made each one had three ships in it at a ranges of 44 and 46 miles. I then passed this information through to Dover Command.'

As Beachy Head was an RAF station, it only reported the aircraft plots through to Fighter Command. Reports of enemy ships were passed to the naval command in whichever command area they were spotted – Portsmouth, Newhaven or Dover. Corporal Jones had trouble sending the shipping sighting through to Dover that morning, for there was no direct line from Beachy Head to Dover; all communications had to be routed via the local Coastguard station and, as it happened, all lines were busy when he tried to pass the message on. Frustrated by the hold up, he made contact with Portsmouth and asked them to forward the sightings on to Dover. Further plots were requested, but continual interference blotted out all other sightings. It was not until 1040hrs that Dover received news of the ships, but even then nobody was aware that they were the German battlefleet, nor was anyone concerned that the continuous interference might actually be enemy jamming of the radar frequencies.

Beachy Head was not the only RDF station that had noticed the circling aircraft, and Fighter Command had also received a few reports of both these aircraft and of the persistent interference. Squadron Leader Davis had come on duty at Fighter Command's HQ at Uxbridge at 0830hrs, and had noticed the plots of enemy aircraft off the coast of France. After several discussions with Air Commodore Norton, the duty commodore at Fighter Command, and with the Controller of No. 11 Group, in whose sector the plots were based, it was decided that a German air/sea rescue was in progress. However, the plots continued over the next hour or so and seemed to be moving along the Channel from west to east. Sometimes the reports showed single aircraft, whilst other times several aircraft were plotted. From 0920hrs reports were also coming in of sporadic and often persistent bouts of interference affecting RDF stations. Davis had a feeling that something unusual was happening and at 1010hrs decided to ask No. 11 Group to send a reconnaissance flight over the area to determine what was going on.

Newhaven RDF combined plotting room was operated by the Army, and came under Brigadier Rawl's IV Corps coastal artillery network. Its first intimation that there was something unusual happening in the Channel came at 1105hrs with a report by station K7 at Fairlight just to the east of Hastings. Its plot showed two large vessels surrounded by several small vessels with an air umbrella over them. The speed of the flotilla appeared to be around 30 knots, much too fast for a conventional convoy. The information was passed through to Dover, who identified the plot as hostile. Reports were also sent to Portsmouth and Fighter Command at Uxbridge. All radar stations along the coast were now alerted to these vessels and ordered to give speed and bearing figures to all services, but enemy jamming prevented any further meaningful plots being obtained.

The special reconnaissance ordered by No. 11 Group was in the air at 1020hrs. It was flown by two Spitfires of 91 Squadron from Hawkinge airfield. Leading the sortie was Squadron Leader Oxspring with Sergeant Beaumont flying with him in the second Spitfire. By this time the weather was closing in with low cloud and squally showers. Visibility was poor when, some 7 miles off Boulogne, Oxspring noticed two lines of E-boats totalling nine craft moving eastwards along the Channel. Then, 3 miles up ahead of him, through the haze, he spotted a great number of ships. There were around 25 of them, with several larger vessels in the middle. The squadron leader decided to go down for a closer look, ever wary of the enemy fighters that were known to be around.

PREVIOUS PAGES
The first few of Oberst Adolf Galland's Fw 109s sweep down over the German warships just after dawn to begin their watchful vigil above the battle fleet. The arrival of the German fighters off the French coast marked the start of the protective air umbrella that was to remain over the Nazi ships through their long voyage up the English Channel and into the North Sea. For the next few hours the German aircraft had little to do, for it was not until they had reached the Straits of Dover that the opposing fighters of the RAF put in an appearance.

Oxspring later described what happened during the descent to get a better look at the enemy ships:

> Our attention was slightly distracted shortly afterwards by our sighting of what we thought were two Me 109s. They were below us and very close to the bunch of E-boats we had seen. We had to keep a very close watch on them because there was also the possibility of being jumped on out of the clouds above us, which were very low and had 10/10ths cover. Enemy fighters could have been hidden in them for they often used two fighters as a decoy. We were rather wary about this, but Beaumont went down to attack one of the two planes below. It was then that we found they were Spitfires, although we had not been told that there were any Spitfires in the area.

The two aircraft pulled out of the dive, slipped back into the clouds and set course for home. Although they had immensely important information to give to their control, standing orders were for complete radio silence. All Oxspring could do was to return to base and report his sightings in person. The pair of Spitfires landed at 1050hrs and the two men sprinted across the airfield to the control tower, where they reported what they had seen out in the Channel to their sector station at Biggin Hill. To them it was a large German naval convoy they had spotted; an important target no doubt and one that would be taken seriously. What they did not know, for no one had told them, was that this could be the German battlefleet that high command had been expecting, although when making his report Beaumont did recall that one of the larger vessels he saw looked as though it had the tripod main mast of a capital ship. Biggin Hill passed the sightings on to No. 11 Group HQ and to the Navy at Dover. Then Fighter Command and the Admiralty received the news, but none of these headquarters were sufficiently convinced that the sightings had actually identified the German heavy ships. As far as anyone was concerned, the enemy big ships were still in Brest and these vessels off Boulogne were just an unusually large convoy.

Oxspring and Beaumont's patrol had by chance almost flown into another friendly flight that was in the air at the same time. These two Spitfires were being flown by Group Captain Victor Beamish and Wing Commander Boyd from Kenley aerodrome. Beamish was Officer Commanding Kenley and Boyd his second-in-command. The two senior officers were aloft that day on what was just a routine sweep of the Channel south of Boulogne. It was not exactly a joy ride, but was a sortie that enabled the station's desk-bound senior officer, Group Captain Beamish, to 'keep his hand in'. Unaware of anything happening in the Channel, Beamish and Boyd were simply looking for some action.

Beamish later described the patrol:

> We took off from Kenley at 1010 hours steering a course over Dungeness for the French coast. We took off through snow; the weather was bad. When in sight of the French coast we saw two Messerschmitts steering SW. We were at sea level; they were at about 1,500 feet. We chased them at full throttle, but did not gain much on them – they were

going very fast. The next thing we saw, at about 1040 hours, was that we were over the fleet. We were about five miles off the French coast near Le Touquet. I saw two ships roughly in line astern, surrounded by around 12 destroyers, circled again by an outer ring of E-boats. When we arrived over the ships we saw in the air around nine to twelve ME 109s. They immediately attacked us.

German anti-aircraft crew on one of the capital ships during the run up the English Channel. (IWM MU4984)

The enemy fighters were 1,000ft above the two Spitfires, and Beamish and Boyd quickly tried to gain height. They both pulled into a sharp turn, hoping to get behind the enemy, but ran into a large amount of enemy anti-aircraft fire from the ships below. Red and green tracers flashed across their path as all the warships' gunners tried to lock onto the swift-moving Spitfires. Whilst taking this evasive action the two pilots managed to get some cannon fire away, aimed at the E-boats below. Some hits were seen, but Beamish realized that the strength of the enemy forces pitted against them required both of them to disappear into the clouds and head for the home base to report their sightings. The enemy fighters declined to follow; their orders required them to remain over the warships as an air umbrella.

Down below in the convoy, Ciliax saw the two Spitfires and realized that his fleet had at last been spotted. It was inevitable that the British now knew their location, course and speed and would soon begin vectoring all their strength to intercept the warships as they passed through the narrow Dover Straits just a few miles ahead of them. Now everyone on board the German ships knew for certain that the main battle would shortly begin.

Beamish and Boyd, like Oxspring and Beaumont before them, headed for Kenley airfield in complete radio silence. They followed standing orders and raced home intent on giving their report in person. The two Spitfires landed at 1109hrs and the pilots sprinted for the nearest telephone to report their sighting of the German battlefleet. By 1111hrs the intelligence officer in the control tower had been given the facts. He passed these on straight away to No. 11 Group at Uxbridge, 31 minutes after the initial sighting had been made by Beamish at 1040hrs. The ban on radio transmissions whilst on patrol had allowed the enemy to sail another 17 miles up the Channel undetected.

There was some later criticism of this radio silence, but the RAF responded with its reasons for insisting on reconnaissance patrols sticking to the policy: 'This prohibition in normal circumstances is perfectly sound, since in the Channel the object of the fighters is to get their report back to headquarters without the enemy realising that they have been seen. There is then a fair chance of the striking force getting over the target before the enemy's air umbrella is in operation.' That was probably true for normal events, but the consequences of the German ships passing unscathed through the Channel were such that this rigid dictate of radio silence should have been broken, especially as such a senior officer had actually made the sighting.

The latest news from Beamish and Boyd, which filtered into all of the command headquarters of the RAF and the Royal Navy, carried more weight than previous reports. A senior RAF officer had identified the warships in the eastern Channel as being the heavy units from Brest. There was now no doubt about it and the codeword 'Fuller' was flashed all along the south coast of England: 'The German ships are out!'

The Channel Coast Guns Open Fire

Confirmation of the start of Fuller resulted in all the formations earmarked for the operation coming into action. Fighter Command, Coastal Command and Bomber Command were alerted and given the speed and position of the enemy so that they could organize their efforts. Nearer to hand, Vice-Admiral Ramsay at Dover had two immediate units with which to attack the enemy, both of which seemed too puny to send against such a powerful enemy force.

At that time in the war, the most useful weapon to have any chance of sinking a major vessel was the torpedo. Ramsay had just two means of launching torpedoes readily available to him. First were the MTBs stationed at Dover and Ramsgate, second were the slow-flying Swordfish biplanes stationed at Manston. None of the better-suited torpedo-carrying Beaufort aircraft were yet in position for action – they were all still in transit to Kent and it would be some time before they could be launched into the attack. Ramsay had to go with what he had ready.

Neither of the two viable options was suitable for daylight attack; both were designed to be used in Operation Fuller in a close-quarters night operation. The MTBs were light inshore craft and were easily outmatched by the faster E-boats that formed a screen around the German battlecruisers. They would be most vulnerable to attack from the air and sea. It was unlikely that any of them would be able to penetrate the E-boat and destroyer screen to get close enough to the big ships to launch their torpedoes effectively, even supposing they were not knocked out by enemy aircraft during their approach. The Swordfish were likewise constrained by their slow speed. They would have to chug along on their bombing run towards the battlefleet at a painfully slow 85 knots, through a barrage of fire that would be so concentrated it would be impossible to escape unscathed. Nonetheless, with grave misgivings, Vice-Admiral Ramsay gave orders for both types of attack to be made.

The enemy ships were now in the waters off Cap Gris Nez opposite the white cliffs, and would soon be within the range of the Channel coast guns near Dover. There were many batteries of coastal artillery around Dover, as there were along the whole of the south coast, but most of these guns were 'fortress' guns, installed to protect ports and naval bases. They were located in positions to counter enemy ships that might attack these areas, and so their range was limited to inshore coastal waters. At Dover these 'fortress' guns, mainly of 6in calibre, had a maximum range of around 20,000yds, well short of the distance required to reach the German ships passing through the Straits. Dover did have larger guns installed for cross-Channel bombardment to counter the German guns installed at Cap Gris Nez, such as the 15in battery at Wanstone, but these guns had a slow rate of fire, a very limited traverse and would be impossible to use against fast-moving ships. The only weapons available that were capable of being used

The now derelict underground plotting room of the South Foreland Battery located on the cliffs to the east of Dover. At the time of the Channel Dash, this room was the centrepiece of activity as the team inside tried desperately to get some positive bearings on the German ships, which were sailing past the battery through the Dover Straits some 15 miles away. (Colin Godfrey, subterraneanhistory.co.uk)

offensively against enemy warships were contained in just one battery of four 9.2in guns at South Foreland. With the guns' effective range of just 31,500yds, there would only be a short period of time when the enemy ships would be within their sights.

The 9.2in guns at Dover were part of IV Corps coastal artillery, commanded by Brigadier Rawl. Those at South Foreland were garrisoned by 350 Battery Royal Artillery. The weapons had not long been installed and their gun crews were still being trained. As part of the battery, a 'K' type radar installation was capable of following targets and able to give continuous range and bearing details. Up until this point, the newly installed radar had not actually been used to control the fire of the guns.

Previously, at 1050hrs, the radar station K7 at Fairlight near Hastings had picked up two ships with air cover off the coast of France, range 67,000yds bearing 136 degrees. This plot was passed to the plotting room at Vice-Admiral Ramsay's headquarters in Dover Castle, and the sighting was logged at 1105hrs. The ships were recognized as being hostile and were given the plot number E29D. No one knew then that they were the German heavy units, but they did appear to be very interesting. Then, at 1129hrs, station K148 at Lydden Spout registered the enemy plot and reported it as being at 46,000yds bearing 166 degrees. A minute later, news arrived that the ships had been positively identified as being the battlecruisers *Scharnhorst* and *Gneisenau* together with 25 other vessels. Straight away the battery of coastal guns at South Foreland near Dover were informed and alerted for action.

Now that the enemy ships had been positively identified, Ramsay was able to give Brigadier Rawl the order for his guns to engage target E29D when ready. The gunners at South Foreland were on practice drill when the order for action was received, and the sound of the klaxon reverberating across the clifftop position sent everybody racing to their stations. Lydden Spout radar station had the target locked on and continued to plot the passage of the enemy ships to feed range and bearing information to the fire command post at South Foreland as the guns were made ready. Within the perimeter of the battery, the shorter-range 10cm 'K' type radar now probed through the mist and gloom searching for its target. At 1203hrs the battery commander, Major Huddlestone, was able to report from his fire control to the Corps Commander Coast Artillery (CCCA) that the guns were ready for action, and Lydden Spout gave the range as 32,000yds. Soon the ships would be within range of the South Foreland guns.

The German ships were now passing through the Straits of Dover and every observation point was full of officers with field glasses trying to spot the enemy. Brigadier Rawl at Dover Castle was peering through his binoculars into the murky weather that covered the straits, but could see nothing. The men manning the optical rangefinders at South Foreland and the battery commander himself all tried in vain to cut through the gloom to locate the enemy, but none could see through the mist and low cloud. At 1212hrs, fresh location, course and speed bearings were fed into the battery plotting room, and at 1215hrs the battery's own radar set picked up the leading target, but the plotters reported that 'the bearing was erratic due to the lack of target discrimination'. The variety of plots being obtained by the radar from the fleet of ships was making it difficult to determine the main target; the range plots agreed with the battery plotting room, but the bearings were uncertain.

With maximum visibility down to just 5 miles, Brigadier Rawl realized that the firing and the 'fall of shot' corrections would have to be done by radar. It was imperative that the impact point of every salvo fired by the guns was located, so that adjustments to the aiming of the weapons could be made continually as the ships passed by. Without this information, the guns could not be effectively ranged onto their target. The problem was that, at this point in time, the process had not been perfected, or indeed even tried.

At 1219hrs South Foreland Battery opened fire with the first hostile response by British armed forces against the German ships since they had left Brest. Ciliax had finally forced his enemy into action. The battery opened up with a half-salvo from two of its guns, although No. 3 gun actually misfired due to a broken lead. No fall of shot was observed from the British side of the Channel. On board the German ships, just 2 miles off the French coast, however, the flash of the guns could be seen though the gloom as they fired, and a period of anxious waiting followed before the shells could be heard screaming their way through the low clouds. But all was well for the Germans, for the shells splashed down harmlessly into the grey-green water more than a mile to port to the rear of the nearest German escort. Orders were now given for the E-boats to make smoke to help screen the fleet from the British shore.

The battery tried again at 1223hrs with another two-gun half-salvo in the hope that its radar would pick up the exploding shells. Nothing was seen on the screens of station K147 alongside the guns. Major Huddlestone tried again four minutes later with the same results; the rumble of exploding shells could be heard, but no comforting further explosions that could indicate a hit. The shells were still falling well astern of the enemy ships.

The station log noted the next move:

> 1228 hours, CCCA decided that as no fall of shot had been observed, the battery should fire 4-gun salvos without waiting for fall of shot observations. Orders given to this effect. Both range and bearing plots agree at the Battery Plotting Room. 1229 hours, battery salvo, no fall of shot observed. 1230 hours, battery salvo. Additional 1,000 yards added as no fall of shot observed.

The only coast guns available to counter the German ships were now firing blind with just hit or miss corrections. It was not surprising that no strikes were made. The barrage continued until 1236hrs when it fired its last salvo at a range of 30,000yds, its shells falling well astern of the last of the major units, the *Prinz Eugen*. The radar tried to vector on the ships following behind, but no positive range or bearings could be obtained. By then the men of 350 Battery had something else to contend with, for just one minute earlier the enemy's coastal guns on Cap Gris Nez began to engage the battery with counterfire, and two Germans shells landed near the observation post.

South Foreland's guns had fallen silent, but the enemy continued firing until 1252hrs, by which time all the German fleet was well out of range of the British guns. Vizeadmiral Ciliax's ships had run the gauntlet of 33 rounds from the British heavy guns and had emerged intact.

The MTB Attack

Out in the Channel, the German boats continued a zigzag course until they were sure they were out of range of the Dover guns. On board the *Prinz Eugen*, the nearest major unit to the shells that had plunged into the sea just to its rear, the gunnery commander, Korvettenkapitän Paulus, watched with satisfaction as the fire from the British heavy guns died away. 'Well,' he remarked to the rangefinder officer standing next to him, 'That wasn't much was it?'

On the admiral's bridge of the *Scharnhorst*, Ciliax was quietly congratulating himself. He could not believe his luck. His ships were through the Dover Straits and all that had been thrown against them was some ineffective and sporadic gunfire. He knew that the British had more than that to send against him, and that the RAF would soon be putting in an appearance in force, but each minute that passed would take his ships closer to more open sea, on which he had more room to manoeuvre. The shallow and confined waters of the English Channel were gradually slipping astern. If the ship beneath him was suddenly sunk even now, he would still go down in history as the first commander in 300 years to lead a hostile battlefleet through the length of the English Channel unscathed.

Lieutenant-Commander Pumphrey was in his office in Dover harbour at 1130hrs. He was writing reports of the day's earlier training practices, when a signal came through from Admiral Ramsay's command post in the castle high above him. He was told that the German battlecruisers were out and he was to get his flotilla of MTBs to sea as quickly as possible. The enemy ships were in the straits just over 20 miles away. It was 1155hrs before Pumphrey led his five serviceable craft out of the harbour and set course to intercept the enemy. The two MGBs also at Dover, there to help protect the MTBs, remained tied up along the ferry quay. Their commanders were absent in the town. Pumphrey left orders for the two officers to be found and return to their craft immediately so as to join up with his flotilla as soon as they could.

In MTB 221, Pumphrey set course to the south-east, trying to intercept the enemy ships. The battlecruisers and their attendant fleet, now numbering almost 60 vessels, had already passed Dover and the MTBs had to steer an intercepting course in order to catch up with them. The British craft would now be forced to approach the enemy ships from the rear on their port flank, provided they could reach them. Pumphrey would now have to attempt to pierce the E-boat screen from the side to get at the major units.

In the original plan for *Fuller*, it was anticipated that the MTBs would be at sea in the Dover Straits under the cover of darkness, waiting for the enemy ships. They would then drive straight at them from the front at their maximum speed, lit from above by flares dropped by the RAF. Above them Beaufort torpedo-bombers would launch their strike on one flank as the Swordfish put in their attack from the other. A combined simultaneous torpedo attack from three quarters would keep the enemy busy, whilst at least a few of the attackers struck home. At 1223hrs on that winter's day this well-laid plan was now just a meaningless paper exercise, for there would be no simultaneous attack by any aircraft, nor would there be any air support – the aircraft earmarked to cover the MTB attack were still on their airfields with their ground crews working feverishly to get them airborne. Pumphrey and his flotilla would have to go it alone; five wooden motor boats against 60 warships.

'We saw the enemy heavy ships coming out of the smoke laid by the "E" boats and I made an enemy report timed at 1223 hours', recorded Pumphrey later. 'When the range was down to about 1,000 yards between us and the "E" boats we started firing at one another. By that time my five boats were very much straggled.' Pumphrey calculated that the range from his MTBs to the battlecruisers was about 5,000yds and decided he needed to get closer.

Pushing his boat to maximum speed, the flotilla leader looked to get ahead of the E-boat screen in order to turn into the capital ships. Just then one of his engines faltered and his speed dropped away. It then misfired to such an extent that he had to signal the others to carry on the attack without him. He was, however, able to turn half to starboard and get one of the battlecruisers, the *Scharnhorst* he thought, into his sights through the screen for long enough to launch his two torpedoes. It was an ambitious attack and one that was almost certainly doomed to fail – no hits were made.

Fairmile Class D Motor Torpedo Boat of the type used against the German capital ships. Its armament – one 2-pdr gun and two 20mm Oerlikon cannons – seemed quite puny when compared with the big guns of the enemy battlecruisers, but its two 21in torpedo tubes could be deadly at close range. (IWM A25315).

The other boats soon found that their speed was insufficient to overhaul the E-boat screen, and so their attacks, like Pumphrey's, would have to be made through the line of enemy craft now opening up with their guns.

As they closed to make their attack, fire from the German vessels increased both in accuracy and intensity, and then German fighter aircraft joined in the battle, strafing the MTBs from low level. The British boats found it very difficult to take both evasive action and to line themselves up with the distant battlecruisers to launch their strikes. The next two craft, MTBs 48 and 219 also fired their torpedoes through the E-boat screen between 1231hrs and 1235hrs from a distance of around 4,500yds. Again no hits were made. The fourth boat in line, MTB 45, also fired through the line, although one of its missiles misfired. This craft was at the end of the E-boat screen near the rear of the fleet of enemy ships. MTB 45's attack attracted the attention of a *Narvik*-class destroyer that was acting rearguard to the fleet, and it pulled out of the line towards the torpedo boat, making smoke to hide the major units as it closed on the small British craft.

The commander of MTB 45 turned towards the destroyer and fired the torpedo that was still in its tube, but again suffered a misfire. With the German ship now bearing down on it, MTB 45 swung round to join the other escaping torpedo boats. Just then the gun boats from Dover made an appearance. MGB 41 and MGB 43 now slipped between the destroyer and the MTBs to engage the German ship and made smoke to cover the escape, using their high speed to evade enemy fire.

The last of the Dover torpedo boats, MTB 44, had been delayed well astern of the rest of the flotilla through an intermittent engine malfunction. It now came up to join in the action. The E-boat screen was well ahead of the vessel and its commander brought the craft to starboard to pass astern of this screen. With the rearmost destroyer out of line chasing the other MGBs, MGB 44 was able to reach a position 2 miles astern of the battlecruisers. Unfortunately the enemy's major units were at the time manoeuvring to evade the tracks of the previously fired torpedoes. At 1235hrs, MTB 44 fired its first torpedo with no observed effects. Five minutes later it closed to 3,000yds and fired its second missile. A large spout of water was seen to rise from the *Prinz Eugen* and it was suspected that a hit had been made, but this proved to be a false sighting. MTB 44 then turned towards home, making to rendezvous with the rest of the flotilla at the SE Goodwin buoy.

The Dover MTBs were not the only torpedo boats to attack that day. Three more MTBs earmarked for *Fuller*, under the command of Lieutenant Long, were stationed at Ramsgate some 12 miles to the north of Dover. Long's MTBs did not get started until 1225hrs, after receiving the signal to attack. When they finally sighted some of the enemy ships through the misty weather, they imagined that they were seeing the leading vessels of the port wing of the destroyer and E-boat screen. Long therefore moved his three craft into a position from which he could attack the major units when they reached him. He was wrong, for his MTBs had crossed astern of the E-boat flotilla and the battlefleet, so that all of the enemy ships were by then well to the north-east of his position, having disappeared into the gloom.

During the latter part of the attack made by the Dover MTBs, some of the enemy's attention had been drawn skywards by another naval attack. Swordfish aircraft of the Fleet Air Arm were launching their own forlorn attempt to torpedo the ships. The same fire that had beaten back the small motor craft also did great damage to the torpedo-bombers, and the scattered MTBs that were still in the area now swung to the north-east to be ready to pick up survivors from any of those aircraft that were unfortunate enough to be shot down into the sea.

The Swordfish Attack

The Fleet Air Arm's 825 Squadron had acquitted itself well during the campaign to sink the *Bismarck* the previous year. Its squadron commander, Lieutenant-Commander Eugene Esmonde, was a very experienced officer who had received a Distinguished Service Order (DSO) for his part in the attack that crippled the German battleship. Since that action, the squadron had been reformed and had seen a number of changes to its composition. It was now really just a half-squadron, for it contained just six fully operational aircraft and included a large number of new recruits.

The squadron had still not reached its full effectiveness when Esmonde was told to fly his squadron from its base at Lee-on-Solent in Hampshire to Manston airfield in Kent as part of the preliminary organization of Operation *Fuller*. The plan required the presence of a squadron of torpedo-carrying Swordfish to be stationed close to the Dover Straits, to take part in the planned mass torpedo attack to be launched against the enemy ships should they try to force their way through the Channel. It was intended that 825 Squadron would attack at night in concert with Beaufort bombers and MTBs.

Although ancient looking and quite obsolete, the Swordfish biplane torpedo-bomber provided a stable platform from which to launch its weapons. It was then the Royal Navy's only torpedo-bomber. Built of light fabric stretched over metal struts with open cockpits, it was operated by a crew of three: a pilot, an observer and a rearwards-facing aerial gunner who manned a swivel-mounted Vickers machine gun. One dubious advantage of the Swordfish was that it could take a great deal of punishment without being destroyed – anti-aircraft shells would often pass through the fabric without exploding. In the era of modern warfare it clearly belonged to a past age, and yet it still appeared to be effective if operated with diversionary support under the cover of darkness.

Whilst Vizeadmiral Ciliax's fleet was sailing unobserved past the coast of Brittany during the early hours of that morning, Esmonde's six aircrews were on full alert by their aircraft, waiting for the possibility of the German ships passing through the Dover Straits in the darkness before dawn. When daylight came without any reconnaissance reports indicating that the German ships had left Brest, all units taking part in *Fuller* were 'stood down' until the next night. Everyone believed that the enemy was evidently not coming through that day.

Esmonde continued with the training of his aircrews during the morning, oblivious to the fact that the enemy's battlefleet was approaching an area of

THE BATTLE OF THE DOVER STRAITS

12 FEBRUARY 1942

The most critical phase of Operation *Cerberus* was the passage of the German ships through the Straits of Dover. This section of the voyage was viewed with great apprehension by the German High Command. It was here that the strongest of Britain's forces would be expected to concentrate against them. Land (coastal artillery), sea and air attacks would be launched towards the battle fleet in these confined waters with little room available to the warships for manoeuvre. Vizeadmiral Ciliax expected that at least one of his ships would be lost within sight of the English coast.

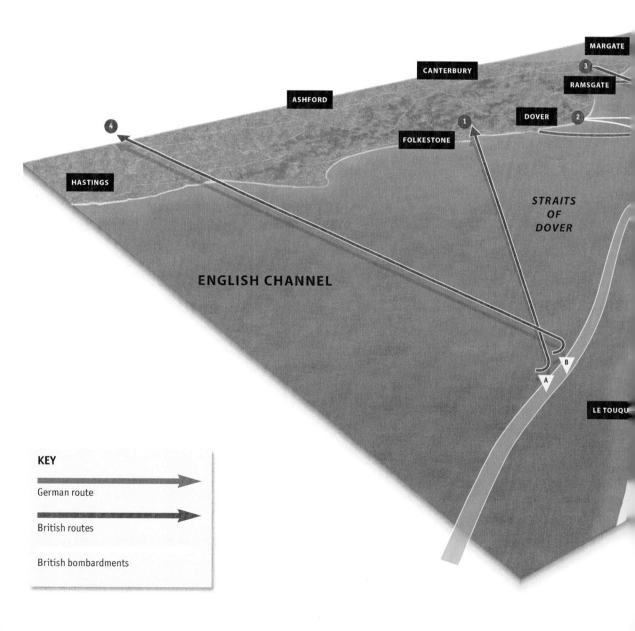

KEY

German route

British routes

British bombardments

BRITISH FORCES

1 Hawkinge airfield
2 South Foreland battery
3 Manston airfield
4 To Kenley airfield

N

DUNKIRK

BELGIUM

CALAIS

FRANCE

Z NEZ

SAINT-OMER

GNE-SUR-MER

ETAPLES

EVENTS

A 1030hrs: German battle squadron sighted for the first time by Squadron Leader Oxspring and Sergeant Beaumont who return to their base at Hawkinge airfield at 1050hrs to report.

B 1040hrs: Group Captain Beamish and Squadron Leader Boyd identify the German ships and return in radio silence to their base at Kenly to report the sighting at 1111 hrs.

C 1219hrs: South Foreland's 9.2in coast guns open fire on the enemy ships.

D 1233hrs: Lieutenant Pumphrey and his Dover motor torpedo boats make contact with the enemy E-boat screen around the German capital ships. Over the next five minutes the MTBs attack the heavy ships with torpedoes, none of which find their target.

E 1236hrs: The South Foreland batteries fire the last of their 33 shells against the German battle squadron as the enemy ships pass out of range. No hits were made.

F 1250hrs: Squadron Leader Esmonde leads his six Swordfish torpedo bombers from 825 Squadron into their attack on the German ships; all of the aircraft are shot down without any of their torpedoes making strikes.

G 1312hrs: Lieutenant Long tries to find the enemy capital ships with his three MTBs from Ramsgate, but can only make contact with the rear of the E-boat screen. The main part of the German battle squadron has passed ahead of him to the north-east.

A flight of nine Swordfish torpedo aircraft on a training sortie over the English coast. (IWM CH626)

the Channel quite close to him. When the Admiralty finally realized that the ships were out, they were actually sailing just 35 miles south of Manston airfield. Admiral Ramsay knew that 825 Squadron had the only aircraft readily available to be launched into the attack, but they were only really effective under the cover of darkness. To send them out in daylight to attack a vast fleet of warships all bristling with anti-aircraft guns, was to send the crews to their certain deaths. Ramsay knew that such an attack would only have a very slim chance of getting close enough to launch a successful strike, but what else was there that could be done? Perhaps to assuage his conscience, Ramsay put a call through to the head of the Royal Navy, Sir Dudley Pound, requesting permission not to have to commit 825 Squadron to such a forlorn endeavour. Pound, ever the traditionalist, reminded Ramsay that 'the Navy will attack the enemy whenever and wherever he is to be found.'

Reluctantly, Ramsay gave the order for the Swordfish attack to go ahead, but was still troubled by what he was asking Esmonde to do. He requested the RAF liaison officer, Group Captain Constable-Roberts, to talk to Esmonde about making the attack and to leave the final decision to the young naval pilot himself. The group captain was put in an unenviable position, for he had to explain to Esmonde that Admiral Ramsay wanted it to be his own personal decision whether or not the attack should go ahead. In effect he was saying to Esmonde that he could pull out of the mission if he wanted to. What could the commander of 825 Squadron do? He could of course back down, but honour and duty would not let him. He would have to do what was expected of him, even with the knowledge that he and his

aircrews were facing almost certain death. Esmonde told Constable-Roberts to let the admiral know that the squadron would go in.

At the same time that Ramsay was alerting those forces under his command, Fighter Command was trying to implement their part in Operation *Fuller* – No. 11 Group was instructed to give fighter escort and cover to the Swordfish attack. Biggin Hill Operations Control telephoned through to Esmonde and outlined its intentions. The airfield would send three squadrons of its fighters across to Manston to rendezvous with 825 Squadron; the Spitfires would act as top cover to keep the *Luftwaffe* from swooping on the Swordfish. Hornchurch Wing would also provide two squadrons of fighters to act as close support to the attack. It was then agreed that at 1225hrs all squadrons would be circling Manston ready to provide cover during the mission. The expected presence of five squadrons of fighters supporting 825 Squadron's bombing run somewhat lessened the hopelessness of the operation. If the enemy was tied up dealing with a massive fighter attack, Esmonde's aircraft might have a better chance of slipping through the expected anti-aircraft barrage, but it was still a tall order.

One by one the elderly Swordfish took off from the seafront runway at Manston and began to orbit the airfield at 500ft, waiting for their fighter escort. The first fighters arrived, flying at 700ft, seven minutes late at 1232hrs; they were from Squadron Leader Kingcome's 72 Squadron from Gravesend, a satellite airfield of Biggin Hill. This was the nearest fighter station to Manston. Kingcome had received his orders to scramble his squadron at 1210hrs and had all his aircraft airborne at 1218hrs. He later

Lieutenant-Commander Eugene Esmonde (second from the left) poses with the crew of his Swordfish torpedo aircraft on the decks of HMS *Ark Royal*. Esmonde had just been awarded the DSO in recognition of his action against the German battleship *Bismarck*. (IWM A5826)

claimed he had arrived over Manston at 1228hrs, just three minutes late. Esmonde continued circling until 1234hrs, but no more fighters arrived. The torpedo squadron commander decided he could wait no longer and, with the enemy ships now just 23 miles off Calais, and moving at almost 30 knots, Esmonde felt it was time to go. He ordered a turn to the north-east and led his six Swordfish into battle. Above them, climbing to 2,000ft, were the ten Spitfires who were to protect him from a barrage the like of which had never been seen before in the Channel.

Kingcome later recalled what happened when he met up with the Swordfish torpedo-bombers:

> Without waiting we went off. We followed them out, and between, I should say, about ten and fifteen miles due east of Dover we found the *Prinz Eugen*. We had to go as slowly as possible, but we kept in touch with the Swordfish until we reached the German ships. I saw one large battleship and between twenty and thirty small vessels. The squadron was then broken up by enemy fighters and there was a general fight after that. They were Focke-Wulf 190s and they were operating in pairs. It was impossible to keep in contact with the Swordfish after that, partly due to the enemy fighters and partly due to the visibility which was very poor.

The two other Biggin Hill squadrons ordered to meet with Esmonde's aircraft over Manston – 124 and 401 Squadrons – both arrived at around 1236hrs, a couple of minutes after the Swordfish had left. They had further to travel than the Gravesend squadron, although they were in the air at the same time between 1218 and 1220hrs. Squadron Leader Duke-Woolley knew that he and his 124 Squadron were going to be late, so he crossed the coast at Deal 6 miles south of Manston, and hoped that he could see the Swordfish on their way out. Unfortunately there was no sign of Esmonde's aircraft and no sightings of the Swordfish were made during the action. Duke-Woolley carried on to the north-east and soon became involved with enemy fighters. It then became a matter of survival rather that a close-support mission.

The two squadrons from Hornchurch Wing that had been ordered to give close support to 825 Squadron were in fact based at one of its satellite stations at Fairlop on the outskirts of London, north of the River Thames. The squadrons were tasked with attacking German ships to suppress anti-aircraft fire, to give the Swordfish more of a chance to penetrate the flak. Neither squadron arrived on time; both claimed that they were just five minutes late and Esmonde's torpedo-bombers had by then left. They therefore crossed the coast and headed out to look for the enemy, but moved too far to the west and could not find the ships. They were then attacked by *Luftwaffe* fighters and became caught up in aerial dogfights. None of the pilots saw anything of the Swordfish aircraft they were ordered to protect.

Whilst the four squadrons of Fighter Command were searching for the Swordfish, Esmonde doggedly continued with his mission, leading the squadron in aircraft W5984. With just the ten supporting Spitfires of 72 Squadron for protection, the fabric-covered bombers shuddered their way slowly through squalls of rain and low cloud. The Spitfire pilots had to use all of their flying skills to keep their speed down and to stay with the painfully slow Swordfish. They had to weave from side to side, then rise up and swoop down to help kill their speed. When the enemy fleet was finally sighted at 1250hrs, the torpedo-bombers slipped down to a height of just 50ft above the spray-capped waves and plodded on at a steady 85 knots. Soon tracer from the anti-aircraft guns on the destroyers screening the battlecruisers snaked out to meet the aircraft. Then larger-calibre guns opened up on the Swordfish, and Me 109s and Fw 190s swooped down from out of the clouds onto the old biplanes. The Spitfires all rose up to meet the enemy, breaking up the attack and chasing them away. The Swordfish bombers were on their own.

Another attack by a fresh group of enemy fighters now descended on the Swordfish, strafing Esmonde's squadron with their machine-gun and cannon fire. They could hardly miss the lumbering biplanes on their first run and their bullets tore through the fabric of the aircraft. None of the hits were fatal, as the torpedo-bomber was able to take this sort of punishment providing that none of the damage was to any of its vital parts or to the crew. The fast-moving German fighters could only get one long burst of fire at the bombers before they overshot and had to come round again. By then some of the other Biggin Hill Spitfires had arrived on the scene from the south and were engaging the enemy fighter umbrella.

Esmonde led the attack with the first sub-flight of three aircraft flying in line ahead. The second sub-flight of three, led by Lieutenant Thompson some 1,000yds behind, approached in 'V' formation. Fighters were again dashing amongst them, this time with flaps and undercarriage down to slow their speed. Sub-Lieutenant Lee was the observer in the Swordfish that followed Esmonde on his attack and later reported on what happened:

> Lieutenant Cdr Esmonde was shot up in the first attack, but continued on in a badly damaged aircraft, the port wing being shot to shreds. The other two aircraft in the sub-flight were also badly damaged, in particular Sub Lieutenant Kingsmill's aircraft, the engine and the port wing of which were alight. We flew in over the destroyer screen and sighted two warships slightly on the port bow. Lieutenant Cdr Esmonde altered course and closed in towards the warships, the rest following.

Lee's aircraft, flown by Sub-Lieutenant Rose, had also been badly hit and its rear gunner, Leading Aircraftman Johnson, killed. Lee tried to take over the gun, but could not move the gunner's body. Esmonde continued trying to keep station in his aircraft whilst weaving to evade enemy fighters, which were coming in one after the other in line astern of the sub-flight. Then a shell hit the lower part of Esmonde's aircraft, shooting most of it away and setting light to the tail plane. For a moment the pilot nearly lost control, but recovered enough to continue closing on the largest of the enemy ships just 3,000yds in front of him. It was clear to those flying behind him that Esmonde himself was now badly wounded. Moments later his torpedo-bomber was hit again, and Swordfish W5984 crashed into the sea.

The intelligence summary written four days after the battle from interviews with survivors recounted the final moments: 'The crew of the following aircraft had the impression from the behaviour of the aeroplane that the pilot had been killed. It cannot be said whether the torpedo had been dropped.' However, accounts of the attack written decades after the action describe Esmonde's aircraft having been struck by a shell from one of the battlecruisers' main guns, and that Esmonde had fired his torpedo before his plane was hit.

Sub-Lieutenant Rose, wounded in the back from shell-splinters, followed his leader through the flak and the fire from enemy fighters. At around 3,000yds distance he launched his torpedo at one of the German heavy units. Seconds later his aircraft was hit again and its petrol tank pierced; fortunately it did not catch fire. The wounded pilot then managed to switch to the reserve tank, but the aircraft gradually lost height as Rose banked away for home. He ditched his aircraft shortly afterwards. Lee was able to get Rose out of the aircraft and into the Swordfish's dinghy before it sank, but the body of the dead gunner went down with the aircraft.

Kingsmill's aircraft, the third in the first sub-flight, met the same fate as the others. With its fabric covering in tatters, torn by continual attacks by enemy fighters and hit by anti-aircraft fire, the aircraft flew doggedly on through smoke, mist and rain with its pilot trying desperately to keep it in the air. At a range of 2,000yds Kingsmill released his torpedo, aiming at what he thought was the *Prinz Eugen*. Then another shell smashed into the aircraft, shearing two cylinders off its radial engine. Power faded dramatically as the sub-lieutenant struggled to keep control of the plane. He banked to port and gradually limped through the continuous enemy flak

An officer on the *Prinz Eugen* watches the attack by Esmonde's Swordfish from the bridge of the heavy cruiser during Operation *Cerberus*. (IWM MH 4993)

to crash-land in the choppy sea. It was with great difficulty that the injured crew escaped the bullet-ridden aircraft. Once in the water they found that their dinghy had been shot full of holes and was useless. They remained adrift in the cold waters until one of Pumphrey's MTBs picked them up.

Of the second sub-flight led by Lieutenant Thompson, little is known. None of the aircrew in the three Swordfish that attacked the enemy heavy ships survived to tell his tale. All nine men were posted as missing with their fates unknown. What is known, however, is that their attacks were as resolute as those in the first waves, for the three Swordfish were seen by a few supporting Spitfire pilots and the crews on the MTBs. All describe the torpedo-bombers as flying through flak at low level towards the enemy. The Swordfish all appear to have been blown to pieces without any trace of the aircraft ever being found.

The torpedoes that had been fired caused little discomfort to those in command of the German squadron – each of them was easily avoided by slight changes of course. On board all of the German ships, the crews were amazed to see the fabric-covered biplanes flying steadily through the terrific barrage that was sent against them. Each man could only be impressed by the bravery shown by their aircrews, who doggedly stuck to their mission through overwhelming odds. It seemed fantastic that these flimsy aircraft were all that Great Britain had available to send against them. Kapitän Hoffmann on the bridge of the *Scharnhorst* was heard to remark: 'The English are now throwing their mothball navy at us.'

12 FEBRUARY 1942

1310hrs The German ships exit the Dover Straits

Attacks by Swordfish Torpedo-Bombers of 825 Squadron

1st Sub-Flight

Aircraft	Crew	Position	Outcome
Swordfish W5984	Lieutenant-Commander Esmonde	Pilot	Killed
	Lieutenant Williams	Observer	Killed
	Petty Officer Clinton	Air Gunner	Killed
Swordfish W5983	Sub-Lieutenant Rose	Pilot	Injured in back
	Sub-Lieutenant Lee	Observer	Uninjured
	Leading Airman Johnson	Air Gunner	Killed
Swordfish W5907	Sub-Lieutenant Kingsmill	Pilot	Injured in foot
	Sub-Lieutenant Samples	Observer	Injured in foot
	Leading Airman Bunce	Air Gunner	Uninjured

2nd Sub-Flight

Aircraft	Crew	Position	Outcome
Swordfish V4532	Lieutenant Thompson	Pilot	Killed
	Sub-Lieutenant Wright	Observer	Killed
	Leading Airman Tapping	Air Gunner	Killed
Swordfish W5985	Sub-Lieutenant Wood	Pilot	Killed
	Sub-Lieutenant Parkinson	Observer	Killed
	Leading Airman Wheeler	Air Gunner	Killed
Swordfish W5978	Sub-Lieutenant Bligh	Pilot	Killed
	Sub-Lieutenant Beynon	Observer	Killed
	Leading Airman Smith	Air Gunner	Killed

By now the enemy battlefleet was well through the Dover Straits and into the North Sea. It had survived its passage up the English Channel and had escaped attacks by coastal guns, MTBs, fighter aircraft and torpedo-bombers. So far the voyage had resembled a training exercise, with all events going strictly according to plan; no damage, no injuries and no disasters. It was all too easy.

In contrast, in England things were not going according to plan. So far Operation *Fuller* had been a disaster for the Royal Navy. Its two attacks had been complete failures, with its MTBs being rebuffed without difficulty and all six of its Swordfish aircraft destroyed along with 13 of the 18 brave men that had flown from Manston airfield early that afternoon. The destroyers at Harwich had been alerted to meet the enemy off the Dutch coast later that afternoon and were at sea, speeding to the point at which they hoped to intercept the enemy. It was now the turn of the RAF's Bomber Command and Coastal Command to salvage something from the disarray that had gone before. Unfortunately, their success rate and efficiency was to mirror that of Britain's Senior Service.

Bomber Command and Coastal Command Attacks

One important component of Operation *Fuller* was the commitment of modern Beaufort torpedo-bombers in conjunction with attacks by Fighter Command whilst the enemy ships were in the confined waters of the English Channel. Delays in sighting the German heavy units had made this impossible and that moment had now passed. The German warships were now steaming into the North Sea. It was not, however, just poor aerial reconnaissance and radar jamming that had prevented the attack going ahead earlier, for even two hours after the official sightings of Admiral Ciliax's ships, Coastal Command's Beauforts were still not ready to attack.

Back on 8 February, the head of Coastal Command, Air Chief Marshal Sir Philip Joubert, had issued a summary which indicated that the German warships were likely to try to force a passage through the English Channel some time after 10 February. In preparation for this eventuality, he gave orders for his Beauforts to be repositioned so as to be within striking distance of the enemy when they came through. Joubert had three squadrons available: 86 Squadron based in the West Country at St Eval in Cornwall; 217 Squadron at Thorney Island near Portsmouth along the Channel coast; and 42 Squadron at Leuchars south of Dundee in Scotland.

The Beauforts at Leuchars were held in readiness for use in Norway, there to join in any naval operation against the *Tirpitz*, should that battleship ever venture out into open water. Joubert had ordered 42 Squadron to come south to Coltishall near Norwich in East Anglia and remain on standby for Operation *Fuller*. Unfortunately the move was dogged by bad luck; heavy snow prevented their leaving Scotland for three days, and it was not until 12 February, the day of the breakout, that they carried out the move. Between 0900 and 0915hrs, Squadron Leader Cliff took off from Leuchars with his 14 serviceable Beauforts and landed at Coltishall between 1130 and 1145hrs. Only 13 aircraft actually made it to the aerodrome – one had gone astray over

the River Humber. The squadron was later plagued by inefficiencies – it was discovered that three of the Beauforts were unarmed and there were no torpedoes at Coltishall, for it was a fighter station. The nearest torpedoes were 140 miles away near Grimsby. They were sent for, but by the time they arrived at the airfield the German ships were safe in their home ports. In the meantime, Cliff was briefed on the operation he would lead later in the afternoon. He was to be joined by some of Coastal Command's Hudson bombers and a fighter escort, to make a concerted bomber/torpedo attack on the German battlefleet. All aircraft were to rendezvous over Manston airfield at 1450hrs.

Cliff and his aircraft later met the Hudson bombers and fighters as planned and set off to find the enemy. Not long into the flight, contact was lost and all the aircraft proceeded independently. The enemy ships were found at a time when a full-scale dog-fight between the RAF and the *Luftwaffe* was going on overhead. A few of the Beauforts managed to attack through very poor visibility, heavy flak and numbers of enemy fighters, but no hits were made on the German warships.

The Thorney Island Beauforts were closest to the enemy when the order came through for 217 Squadron to scramble. These torpedo-bombers were ordered to meet with a fighter escort above Manston at 1330hrs. Unfortunately, only four of the seven torpedo-bombers based there were immediately available – three were on two hours notice for service and were not armed with torpedoes. There was then some delay whilst the three were made ready. Eventually, in view of the urgency of the situation, the four

The flash of the main guns of the heavy cruiser *Prinz Eugen* illuminate the ship's smaller-calibre anti-aircraft guns during a British attack in the Dover Straits. (IWM MH 4998)

12 FEBRUARY
1942

1432hrs
Scharnhorst
hits a mine and is
forced to stop

serviceable Beauforts were ordered to take off, and at around 1325hrs they left for Manston to meet up with the Spitfire squadron earmarked to protect them. The others were to follow when they were ready. Whilst the Thorney Island aircraft were on passage, their fighter escorts circled Manston airfield looking for them.

Some control was later established when it was suggested that to save time the fighters would rendezvous with the Beauforts over the target. This message, however, did not get through to the Thorney Island torpedo-bombers. On their arrival over Manston some 20 minutes after their rendezvous time, they began circling the station looking for their escort. When the Spitfires failed to arrive, the Beauforts flew out to sea seeking their target, making for the last-known position given to them an hour earlier at Thorney Island. The Beauforts arrived over an area 50 miles to the rear of the German ships and found nothing. The remaining aircraft that had been left at their home base also arrived over empty skies above Manston. After circling for some time they landed and their pilots went to the control room to ask for instructions. They were given the latest positions of the German ships and took off to attack. They eventually did find the warships at around 1545hrs, the same time that Fighter Command was in contact with the *Luftwaffe* over the ships. The Beauforts swooped down almost to sea level through dense anti-aircraft fire and dropped their torpedoes, but no hits were made.

At the other end of the south coast, Wing Commander Flood was ordered, at 1220hrs, to take all his St Eval Beauforts immediately to Thorney Island. Flood had under his command both his own 86 Squadron (ten serviceable out of a full complement of 18) and a detachment of seven Beauforts from

This photograph, taken from onboard the *Scharnhorst,* shows the *Gneisenau* to its immediate rear with the *Prinz Eugen* further behind. The ships are in the English Channel and the *Prinz Eugen* is firing its main weapons against Esmonde's attacking Swordfish torpedo aircraft. (IWM MH 4981)

217 Squadron, of which five were serviceable, giving a final total of 15 airworthy Beauforts. Three of these, however, were already out on an anti-shipping operation in the Bay of Biscay, so only 12 torpedo-bombers actually left for Thorney Island. They flew in two groups of six and all were on the coastal airfield in Hampshire by 1415hrs. After refuelling, Flood's torpedo-bombers were ordered to fly on to Coltishall. At 1700hrs they were to rendezvous with a fighter escort over the airfield. This combined force was then to make for the sea area off Walcheren near the Dutch coast. It was estimated that the enemy ships would be in this position at around 1745hrs.

When the Beauforts arrived at Coltishall airfield, they found no fighter escort waiting for them and no sign of fighters on the ground. They circled the aerodrome waiting for Fighter Command's long-range Spitfires to show up, but the fighters did not arrive. As light was now fading, Flood made the decision at 1705hrs to lead his Beauforts out into the North Sea and try to intercept the enemy at the estimated location given to him by his control. His mission was a failure. Visibility was poor, with cloud cover at 1,000ft, sometimes descending to 600ft. Other than three German minesweepers, he saw nothing. Flood ordered his flight to disperse and look for the capital ships, but although two aircraft were lost to some sort of enemy fire, the battlecruisers eluded them.

Bomber Command had an acting commander in place that day. Air Vice-Marshal Baldwin was in post waiting for the new commander, Air Marshal Arthur Harris, to arrive back from the United States. Harris would be replacing Air Marshal Sir Richard Peirse, who had led Bomber Command since October 1940 and had left to take up the role of Air Officer Commanding (AOC), Air Forces in India. Baldwin was alerted to the arrival of the German battlecruisers in the Channel at 1145hrs, just five minutes after his controller had agreed with Fighter and Coastal Commands, and with the Admiralty, that *Fuller* was now in operation. All RAF groups had been warned and were told to bring their aircraft to immediate action. Baldwin then contacted each individual group commander and arranged for the first attack to be airborne at 1330hrs.

Each commander gave figures for the number of aircraft that would be ready to take part in this first wave. Bomber Command had around 100 aircraft on four hours notice, bombed up and with their crews on station, but Baldwin was calling for the first attack to be made as soon as possible within two hours. Bomber Command managed to get 73 bombers into this first wave: No. 1 Group had 25 ready, all Wellingtons; No. 2 Group put up 25 Blenheims; No. 4 Group sent ten Wellingtons; and No. 5 Group provided 11 Wellingtons and two Manchesters. No. 3 Group did have aircraft available, but as they consisted mainly of Stirling and Halifax heavy bombers, Baldwin decided to hold these back for the moment. The first attack would be within the range of fighter protection, so he kept his heavies for the later attacks when the enemy had passed out of the range of the fighters.

Bomber Command's first attack on the enemy ships got underway as planned and, after forming up into sections, the aircraft arrived over the estimated position of the German battlecruisers at around 1430hrs.

Unfortunately, cloud cover was almost 10/10ths, and simply finding the ships proved to be extremely difficult. The cloud ceiling was often as low as 600ft with visibility less than 1,000yds, and the bombers had to descend to almost sea level before they could see anything. Problems were also encountered from the freezing conditions, with windscreens icing up as the aircraft flew through the cold, wet clouds. Not surprisingly, none of the aircraft that returned claimed to have spotted any sign of the enemy convoy. Casualties were high for such a disappointing attack; five aircraft were lost in this first wave. Some aircraft most likely did find the ships, for a few appear to have been shot down; other bombers went too low and hit the sea.

The second wave of bombers, 100 aircraft in total, consisted of 35 Wellingtons, 13 Manchesters and five Halifaxes from No. 5 Group; 29 Wellingtons and two Stirlings from No. 3 Group; and 12 Wellingtons and four Bostons from No. 2 Group. The aircraft were over the target at 1630hrs, with results that were even worse than the first raid: nothing found and nine aircraft lost. They had set off flying in sections, but order was soon lost and each aircraft gradually became separated from its companions. Bombers eventually attacked singly, flying backwards and forwards through thick cloud and rain squalls trying to find their targets. The mission became a long drawn-out test of endurance that continued on and off until 1800hrs.

The third wave consisted of just 41 bombers, mainly Stirlings and Halifaxes from No. 5 Group, with some Wellingtons from No. 2 Group. These aircraft arrived over the target area at the same time as the stragglers

Ground crew manoeuvre a number of torpedoes in front of a Beaufort torpedo-bomber of RAF 22 Squadron. (IWM 1854)

from the second wave were still trying to get into position to drop their bombs. By this time, the supporting fighters had all reached the limits of their operational range and had returned to base. Those aircraft of the third wave that managed to arrive at the enemy's estimated position began flying over the target at 1745hrs and remained in the area until 1815hrs. Few aircraft found the enemy ships and those that did had difficulty bombing effectively. One bomber was lost on this last effort.

On board the German ships, the anti-aircraft crews remained at their stations throughout the day. Bombers could be heard overhead, but few swooped down out of the clouds to make an attack. Those that did were generally forced away by the large volume of flak thrown up against them. Kapitän Hoffmann on the *Scharnhorst* was never sure if the British aircraft that came over during this four-hour period were from new waves or whether it was just the same bombers repeatedly circling around, trying to find his ship.

The attacks by Bomber Command, although pressed home by determined and skilful aircrews, achieved nothing. Their presence over the German fleet concentrated the attention of the ship's crews and required some changes of course and much anti-aircraft fire, but ultimately did very little to alarm Vizeadmiral Ciliax and those in command of his ships. In total, Bomber Command flew 398 missions that day, lost 17 planes and had more than 20 damaged. The effectiveness of bombers against warships, especially in low cloud, was particularly disappointing. What made it more so was the fact that even if any of them had scored a direct hit on any of the warships, those at the top of Bomber Command already knew that they would be ineffective. The bombers carried a mixture of high-explosive general-purpose and armour-piercing bombs. During the subsequent enquiry into the failure of Operation *Fuller*, Baldwin admitted that general-purpose bombs dropped from a low altitude, set with instantaneous fuses, 'would most likely disintegrate or bounce off when they hit anything solid, unless we were lucky enough to get one down the funnel.' He also admitted that armour-piercing bombs had to be dropped from a height of at least 7,000ft to be effective. In fact, all that the head of Bomber Command expected from his bombers was that they might 'distract the attention of the warships and act as cover for the torpedo and destroyer attacks.' This was a shocking admission to make, especially as it was the fear of bombs that had prevented the Admiralty allowing its capital ships to be used in Operation *Fuller*.

The Destroyer Attack

Earlier that day, Captain Pizey, Commander of 21st Destroyer Flotilla, was at sea with the six Harwich-based destroyers that had been allocated to Operation *Fuller*. His force consisted of two elderly destroyers from his flotilla – *Vivacious* and his own ship *Campbell* – and those of the 16th Destroyer Flotilla under Captain Wright: *Mackay*, *Worcester*, *Whitshed* and *Walpole*. The ships had been on immediate notice for action during the expected crucial period before dawn. With no alarm sounded at daylight, the destroyers resorted to normal duties and proceeded out of port on exercises.

12 FEBRUARY 1942

1600–1800hrs The main Beaufort torpedo-bomber force and the aircraft of Bomber Command attack

At 1156hrs, Pizey received a signal from Vice-Admiral Dover that the enemy battlecruisers were in the Channel. At that time, his ships were widely dispersed carrying out independent torpedo and gunnery exercises. Pizey immediately signalled to his destroyer captains to rendezvous near No. 53 buoy, some 20 miles east-south-east of Harwich. The speed of the enemy was estimated at 20 knots, which would give Pizey's destroyers ample time to reach the assembly area and then proceed to the spot planned for the interception.

Unfortunately, the enemy's speed had been underestimated and by 1300hrs it was clear that the destroyers could not cut off the enemy by travelling to the south-east to meet them. The only likely chance of intercepting the enemy ships was to steer eastwards and try to meet them somewhere off the mouth of the River Maas. There was, however, a large problem with this move, for a wide minefield ran across their intended route. Pizey decided, quite bravely, to sail directly through the mine barrier and hope for the best.

By 1318hrs, all ships had closed up in station. Speed was increased to 28 knots and the destroyers turned onto a bearing that would bring them to a position to intercept the Germans at around 1530hrs. Minutes later, the main engine bearings of the *Walpole* began giving trouble, forcing it to drop well astern of the flotilla. It soon became obvious that the destroyer could take no part in the action and it returned to Harwich. Meanwhile, overhead, an enemy Ju 88 had found the task group and began to shadow the ships, even putting in several ineffectual bombing runs as the destroyers raced eastwards. At 1430hrs Pizey's ships had cleared the mine barrier.

Some distance away to the south-west, the German ships were ploughing their way steadily through gathering seas. However, the good fortune that had followed Vizeadmiral Ciliax and his ships since leaving Brest came to an abrupt halt at 1432hrs in the shallow waters off the mouth of the River Scheldt. The *Scharnhorst* was suddenly rocked by a violent explosion; all the lights failed and the battlecruiser began losing way. The ship had hit a mine dropped sometime previously by the RAF.

Those aboard the *Gneisenau* and *Prinz Eugen*, following close behind, were shocked to see Ciliax's flagship sheer off to starboard belching black smoke and leaking oil. Unable to stop – the two heavy ships had to obey the order that they were to keep going even if one of the trio was sunk or damaged – they raced past the stricken battlecruiser and soon disappeared into the mist and rain.

On the bridge of the *Scharnhorst*, Hoffmann was soon given details of the damage: two double compartments flooded and the ship holed on the starboard side. Ciliax heard the news with some alarm and quickly decided he could no longer command the operation from the stricken ship. He ordered destroyer Z.29 to come alongside and take him off, transferring his flag to this smaller ship. It was light and fast and would quickly overhaul the two heavy ships, which were now some miles ahead of him. Ciliax swiftly disembarked onto Z.29 and left Hoffmann and his crew to their fate. Staying behind to render some assistance and protection to the battlecruiser were just four German torpedo boats: *T13*, *T15*, *T16* and *T17*.

The *Prinz Eugen* ploughs through heavy seas in the wake of the *Gneisenau* during Operation *Cerberus*. The *Scharnhorst* is some way ahead of these two warships, and the destroyer and E-boat screen, which was tightly alongside during the passage through the English Channel, has now moved further out as the battlefleet moves through the North Sea.
(IWM HU37542)

This was the situation that the crews of all the German ships had dreaded since leaving port. The great warship was now dead in the water, at the mercy of any British aircraft that might appear in the sky above. If it were attacked by torpedo-bombers or British destroyers, the chances of escaping further damage were minimal. Everyone now waited for Chief Engineer Kretschmer and his men to do their work and try to get the ship moving again.

As the minutes ticked by, their luck held, for no British aircraft came over at what would have been a most opportune moment. The RAF and the Beauforts of Coastal Command were then attacking the main part of the battlefleet situated miles away to the north. At 1449hrs news came from the engine room that the boilers were operating again. Five minutes later, Kretschmer reported to his captain that the port engine shaft was now working. By 1500hrs, the ship was once again underway, making 27 knots in an effort to catch up with the rest of the fleet, which was now some 17 miles ahead of it.

As the focus of attention had moved from the Channel to the north-east, command of the British naval operation had been taken over from Dover by Commander-in-Chief Nore, Admiral Sir George Lyon, at 1411hrs. There was still no accurate position known for the enemy ships, for the shadowing aircraft allocated to track their progress had lost them. Captain Pizey's destroyers were aiming for an approximate position based on last-known reports and the enemy's estimated speed. The captain was now told that if he could not find the enemy by 1515hrs, he was likely to be to the north-east of them and should sweep towards the south-west. He received this signal just at the moment that two large echoes were detected on *Campbell*'s Type 271 radar set. It showed ships 9½ miles distant, passing from right to left on a slowly converging course. Two minutes later, further echoes confirmed that the destroyers had found the enemy battlefleet.

Visibility through the mist and rain squalls was around 4 miles, so Pizey estimated that he would at least have cover for the initial part of his approach. He planned to try to gain some leeway on the enemy before turning to starboard to launch his torpedoes. The destroyers would attack in two divisions, with *Campbell*, *Vivacious* and *Worcester* in the first division and *Mackay* and *Whitshed* in the second.

As the destroyers closed on the enemy, great numbers of aircraft came dipping down out of the clouds; some were friendly, some were not. Their arrival coincided with attacks by both Bomber and Coastal Commands with Beauforts, Hampdens and Wellingtons, which mixed with enemy Me 109s, Ju 88s and Me 110s. Some German pilots thought that Pizey's flotilla was friendly and fired off recognition signals; some British pilots thought it was hostile and tried to bomb it.

The Royal Navy destroyer HMS *Campbell* which, under the command of Captain Pizey, led the 16th and 21st Destroyer Flotilla's attacks on the German ships in the North Sea. (IWM 7479)

At 1542hrs, gun flashes and anti-aircraft fire were seen to starboard bearing 155 degrees, followed a minute later by sightings of the enemy ships some 4 miles distant, which were proceeding in line ahead with their destroyer escort to port. The British destroyers immediately turned to attack, with Pizey's ship leading his division. As they increased speed to close on the German ships as rapidly as possible, all the enemy vessels opened up with their main armament. Pizey ordered ships to zigzag to try to dodge the German salvoes. Very soon the destroyers were straddled by shells of all calibres.

The British replied with their own weapons, hoping to score some chance hits on the enemy. Captain Pizey later described the attack:

> At 3,500 yards I felt that our luck could not hold much longer. Ships were being well straddled and we were closing fast, gradually loosing our bearing. At 3,300 yards I saw a large shell, which failed to explode or ricochet, dive under the ship like a porpoise and I felt this was time to turn and fire our torpedoes. *Vivacious* on my starboard quarter turned and fired at the same time.

After releasing their torpedoes the two ships turned away and retired from the action. Behind them *Worcester* continued to close on the enemy and fired its torpedoes at 4,000yds range. By then the target ships were themselves taking evasive action, turning away from torpedoes launched by *Campbell* and *Vivacious*, so that all the torpedoes fired missed the battlecruisers. Up until then, the destroyers were unscathed, but *Worcester*'s luck then ran out. As it changed course away from the enemy it was struck by a salvo of heavy shells. Hit in Boiler Rooms 1 and 2, it stopped dead in the water. The destroyer now drifted beam on to the sea with its port side exposed to the enemy guns. It was then subjected to four full salvoes of heavy guns, taking a terrible pounding. Fires broke out all over the ship as it began to settle. Soon the forepeak, forward boiler room, wardroom, after magazine and shell room all became flooded. *Worcester* was so badly damaged it seemed impossible that the destroyer could remain afloat. Its captain, Lieutenant-Commander Coats, gave instructions to prepare to abandon ship.

Meanwhile the second division destroyers were attacking the enemy. *Mackay* and *Whitshed* were heading straight for the *Prinz Eugen*. They closed on the enemy without attracting fire from the big guns, the captain of the German heavy cruiser not sure if the destroyers approaching him were friend or foe. At 4,000yds the *Mackay* fired its torpedoes, forcing the *Prinz Eugen* to make a drastic alteration to starboard to avoid being hit. A few cables to the rear, the *Whitshed*'s crew found it difficult to keep their weapons trained on the evasive enemy ship and its captain, Lieutenant-Commander Juniper, had to close to 3,000yds range before he could release his torpedoes. All of the shots could be seen running fast and true, but all missed their target.

A few miles astern, the blazing *Worcester* was wallowing out of control in the heavy seas. The shelling from the enemy had gradually lessened and finally stopped as the ships of the German battlefleet regained their stations and disappeared into the mist and rain; all were hell-bent on escaping to

12 FEBRUARY
1942

1955hrs
Gneisenau
hits a mine

12 FEBRUARY
1942

2135hrs
Scharnhorst hits a
second mine

The Royal Navy's 16th Destroyer Flotilla at sea. The picture shows HMS *Whitshed* with HMS *Walpole* to the rear. (IWM A17925)

their home ports rather than stopping to fight. Much to everyone's surprise the *Worcester* remained afloat. Help was soon to hand when *Campbell* and *Vivacious* altered course to come to her aid. The wounded were taken off, and damage-repair teams got control of the fires and began making the ship seaworthy. Coats refused an offer of a tow by the captain of the *Campbell* for one of her boilers had begun working and steam was now available. He thought that the ship could, with luck, make eight knots. Just then Admiral Lyon ordered all destroyers back to Harwich to reload with torpedoes, to be ready to follow the enemy in chance that one of the German squadron had been damaged and had slowed down.

The *Worcester* bravely limped back to port through gradually worsening seas. From time to time it broke down and was forced to stop for further repairs. By the end of the day, it could barely make 3 knots and it took until dawn the next day before it was safely tied up alongside the quay at Harwich.

The destroyer attack, like all other attacks that day, had failed. Seven old warships had been pitted against an enemy almost ten times their size, with great expectations, but with no realistic chance of success. It was further proof that Operation *Fuller* was a complete shambles. The enemy ships had escaped their pursuers and were now, as daylight faded, well to the north of all British efforts aimed against them.

AFTERMATH

Vizeadmiral Ciliax in *Z.29* did not immediately find the rest of his fleet, for after darkness had fallen the ships had all become separated. The *Gneisenau* and the *Prinz Eugen* had parted company in poor visibility and continued independently. Further misfortune overtook Ciliax when *Z.29* stopped after it suffered major damage to an oil line through a shell misfire. Once again the German commander found himself having to transfer between ships, this time to another destroyer, the *Hermann Schoemann*. He was onboard this ship when it was almost run down at 1816hrs by the *Scharnhorst* as it loomed out of the darkness.

The ships had by then reached the channel off Texel in the Frisian Islands and began to swing round further to the north-east. Soon they would be running due east across the north coast of Holland towards the German ports. There was some comfort to be had onboard the ships from the fact that the British were now left far behind. A very dark night made observation almost impossible. The ships' crews knew that they could now only be found by radar. Even if the RAF did discover them, there was little to fear, for its bombers could not hit them even in daylight. There remained, however, the ever-present danger from mines.

Mines were indeed a threat, for the RAF had been busy along this part of the Dutch coast, laying mines from aircraft in the path of the German ships. The fast minelayer *Welshman* had also been busy sowing the area with even more mines as a precursor to Operation *Fuller*. These mines found an important victim when, at 1955hrs, the *Gneisenau* succumbed to an underwater explosion off the Dutch island of Terschelling. One engine shut down immediately from the effects of the blast and Kapitän Fein ordered the other engines to stop whilst engineers assessed the damage. The *Gneisenau* had been holed on the starboard side, but other damage seemed to be minimal. It took just 30 minutes to repair the hole with a collision mat and resume the passage. Not far away, making the same dangerous passage through the shallow waters, was the *Prinz Eugen*. It was more fortunate than the other two major units, for it made

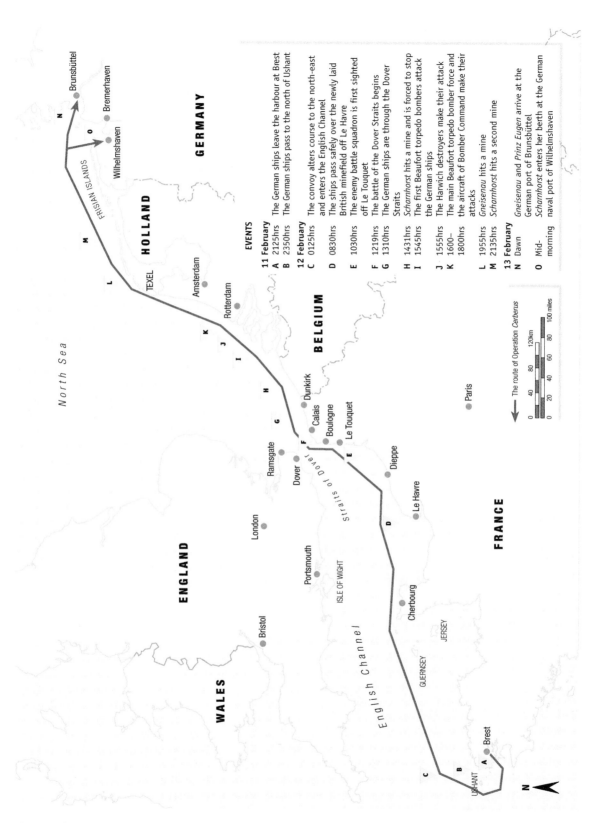

EVENTS

11 February

A 2125hrs The German ships leave the harbour at Brest
B 2350hrs The German ships pass to the north of Ushant

12 February

C 0125hrs The convoy alters course to the north-east and enters the English Channel
D 0830hrs The ships pass safely over the newly laid British minefield off Le Havre
E 1030hrs The enemy battle squadron is first sighted off Le Touquet
F 1219hrs The battle of the Dover Straits begins
G 1310hrs The German ships are through the Dover Straits
H 1431hrs *Scharnhorst* hits a mine and is forced to stop
I 1545hrs The first Beaufort torpedo bombers attack the German ships
J 1555hrs The Harwich destroyers make their attack
K 1600– 1800hrs The main Beaufort torpedo bomber force and the aircraft of Bomber Command make their attacks
L 1955hrs *Gneisenau* hits a mine
M 2135hrs *Scharnhorst* hits a second mine

13 February

N Dawn *Gneisenau* and *Prinz Eugen* arrive at the German port of Brunsbüttel
O Mid- morning *Scharnhorst* enters her berth at the German naval port of Wilhelmshaven

The route of Operation *Cerberus*.

its way through the hastily sown minefields and proceeded unscathed into German waters.

At 2135hrs off the same island of Terschelling, misfortune again struck the *Scharnhorst*. The ship hit another mine and was once more rendered dead in the water. This time the damage was much more severe. The battlecruiser began taking on thousands of tons of water. Its starboard engine was damaged and the other two were jammed. All electrical equipment had failed, instruments were damaged beyond repair by the shock waves and the dynamo room was put out of action. The ship was stationary in darkness with no electrical equipment working and without any means of communication. It was also toothless, for its main armament was inoperable.

Once again Chief Engineer Kretschmer and his team were soon busy sorting out the myriad of problems that had befallen the ship in order to get *Scharnhorst* underway again. After 35 minutes, the redoubtable engineer was able to report to a delighted Kapitän Hoffmann that although the rudder was damaged, and some of the mounting bolts had been wrenched off the starboard engine, he could get both propellers turning to give a speed of some 14 knots. By 2215hrs, the great battlecruiser was underway again.

By the end of that epic day, the three great warships had reached German waters. Just after midnight, *Gneisenau* and *Prinz Eugen* made contact and escorted each other towards the small German port of Brunsbüttel at the southern end of the Kiel Canal on the banks of the River Elbe. They arrived just before dawn and waited for daylight before they manoeuvred through

The *Prinz Eugen* fires its secondary armament at bombers circling above the warship. Most of the RAF bombers failed in their attempts to find and attack the German heavy cruiser whilst it was in the North Sea. (IWM HU35746)

13 FEBRUARY 1942

Dawn
Gneisenau **and**
Prinz Eugen
arrive at
Brunsbüttel

HMS *Worcester* shows some of the damage done to her by the German warships during the afternoon attack in the North Sea. The destroyer was peppered by exploding shell fragments as well as having received direct hits to some of its vital compartments. The crippled vessel managed to limp back to port at Harwich early the next day at a top speed of just 4 knots. (IWM CL5861)

the main lock into the Kaiser Wilhelm Canal to berths especially prepared for their arrival in the north chamber. The *Scharnhorst* took longer to get home and arrived at the naval port of Wilhelmshaven later that morning.

The German battlefleet was now in the relative safety of home ports, to the jubilation of all of Germany. The crews had braved the closed waters of the English Channel, defying both the Royal Navy and the RAF, and had escaped virtually unscathed. Not since the 17th century had an enemy fleet successfully sailed through this stretch of water. It was a naval disaster of the greatest magnitude for the British.

CONCLUSION

When news of the escape of the German ships was made public, there was a national outcry in Britain. The newspapers all asked why such a thing was allowed to happen. How could an enemy fleet successfully sail up the English Channel without even one ship being sunk or damaged? What was the point of having the most powerful navy in the world if it could not stop hostile ships pushing through its front door? The clamour for someone to be blamed for the outrage grew to such an extent that the Prime Minister was obliged to arrange for a judicial inquiry to look into what went wrong.

Just a week after the enemy ships had sailed through the Channel, a panel of three men was assembled to take evidence with regard to the conduct of the individuals and formations involved in the event. Under the presidency of a High Court judge, Mr Justice Bucknill, a board was formed composed of Air Chief Marshal Sir Edgar Ludlow-Hewitt, the Inspector-General of the RAF, and Vice-Admiral Sir Hugh Binney, representing the Royal Navy.

The board interviewed as many of the participants of Operation *Fuller* as possible during the weeks of enquiry, questioning a wide range of service personnel from sergeant pilots to air chief marshals and naval air crew to admirals. Although the board was given a brief to look into what went wrong, the outcome, by necessity, had to be a complete 'whitewash'. The circumstances of war dictated that the nation's arms could not be seen by the public to be incompetent. A fudge was silently agreed, which basically said, barring a few unforeseen errors, all was done that could have been done. The disaster was caused by not identifying soon enough that the Brest ships were out and in the Channel, and all plans were designed around the German ships passing through the Straits of Dover at night. The main failure could be put down to the bad luck of having a blown fuse and damp plugs in some of Coastal Command's reconnaissance aircraft, which were responsible for spotting that the breakout had taken place. Even with these innocuous findings, the report was still deemed to be too sensitive to be published in wartime, so its general release was delayed for four years until 1946, long after the event had faded from memory.

Grossadmiral Raeder accompanies Vizeadmiral Ciliax in reviewing the crew of the *Scharnhorst* in Germany after Operation *Cerberus*. The return of the battlefleet to home ports was a major propaganda coup for the Nazis. It showed that meticulous planning and great determination could triumph over seemingly insurmountable odds. (IWM HU 40195)

Over on mainland Europe, and indeed around the world, the dash through the English Channel was seen as a great German victory. It was a bold and carefully planned operation that showed the indefatigable spirit of the officers and men of the *Kriegsmarine* and their comrades in the *Luftwaffe*. It also demonstrated that Britain was capable of being outwitted on its own doorstep. Perhaps it was not the great power that it imagined itself to be.

In Germany, the returning sailors were feted as heroes. Decorations and awards were given to those prominent in the planning and execution of Operation *Cerberus*. The architect of the breakout had also been proved right. Hitler had been shown to be correct in thinking that the British were incapable of reacting quickly enough to stop the battlefleet passing through the English Channel. The success of the mission strengthened his low opinion of his enemy and reinforced his own belief in himself as a great military commander.

The Channel Dash was a great German victory, or was it? Certainly Operation *Cerberus* achieved its primary goal of returning the battlefleet back to its home ports, but it also finally freed the British from the spectre of having the German ships overlooking its important sea lanes to the west and south. Once the three warships were at rest in Germany, they no longer posed an immediate threat. To be of any use to the Nazis, they had once again to break out. This time the only route was to the north, into an area powerfully guarded by the Royal Navy's Home Fleet. The German ships had exchanged one prison for another. Strategically, the Channel Dash proved to be a victory for the British, for the three capital ships never again sailed together as a strike force.

Operation *Cerberus* was the last victory for the *Scharnhorst*, *Gneisenau* and the *Prinz Eugen*, for their ultimate fates were quite tragic. As soon as the ships had been tied up safely in port, the bombers of the RAF started paying nightly visits to them. Between 25 and 27 February, three particularly heavy raids damaged the *Gneisenau* beyond repair. It never put to sea under its own power again, but was towed to Poland for use as a block ship. Its heavy guns were removed and used in coastal defence works in Norway and Poland.

The *Prinz Eugen* did put to sea again. Just over a week after the dash through the Channel, it was ordered to move to Norway to join the *Tirpitz*. On 23 February the ship was attacked by RAF bombers and torpedo aircraft and badly damaged. It managed to avoid complete destruction and find a safe anchorage for a short while, but never again took part in any operational sorties during the war. The ship ended its days in the charge of the US Navy, and was used in atomic weapons tests in the Pacific.

The *Scharnhorst* at least died a noble death. On 26 December 1943, it took part in the battle of the North Cape off Norway and was sunk by the capital ships of the British Home Fleet. It went to the bottom along with most of its 1,970 crew. Just 36 survivors were rescued from the icy Arctic waters.

13 FEBRUARY 1942

Mid-morning *Scharnhorst* enters Wilhelmshaven

SOURCES AND FURTHER READING

A number of books have been written in connection with the Channel Dash, the most informative of which are listed below. There also exists, at The National Archives at Kew in London, the papers relating to the Board of Inquiry into the event. These interviews were used in the production of the Bucknill Report. The files contain the testimonies of many of the people questioned during the inquest into the incident. Direct quotations from the participants contained in this book are taken from these Crown Copyright archives. As the participants were questioned within days and weeks of the operation, their memories of what happened were quite clear. Interviews with these people for later publications often showed quite different narratives. For instance, in one interview with a particular squadron leader, conducted some 20 years after the war, he claimed that he saw the end of several of the Swordfish aircraft. In the statement he made just after the operation, he reported that he saw nothing more of the Swordfish once he was engaged with enemy fighters, but *one of his pilots* saw a Swordfish crashing into the sea.

Selected Published Titles

Busch, Fritz-Otto, *The Drama of the Scharnhorst*, Robert Hale, London (1956)

Busch, Fritz-Otto, *The Story of the Prince Eugen*, Robert Hale, London (1958)

Cameron, Ian, *Wings of the Morning*, Hodder & Stoughton, London (1962)

Deane Potter, John, *Fiasco*, Heinemann, London (1970)

Robertson, Terence, *Channel Dash*, Evans, London (1958)

Records held at The National Archives, Kew

ADM 1/20126   Inaccuracies contained in Bucknill Report

ADM 116/4528   Board of Inquiry evidence

ADM 199/620   Destroyer attempts to intercept German battlecruisers *Gneisenau*, *Scharnhorst* and *Prinz Eugen*

ADM 234/328   Passage of enemy fleet through English Channel and report of operation in Battle Summary 11

AIR 20/3061   Admiral Ramsay's report

AIR 16/899   Passage of *Scharnhorst* and *Gneisenau* through the Channel and report by Flight Lieutenant Kidd

AIR 2/7912   Passage of the *Scharnhorst*, *Gneisenau* and *Prinz Eugen* through the Straits of Dover (Board of Inquiry evidence)

AIR 8/614   RAF attacks on *Scharnhorst*, *Gneisenau* and *Prinz Eugen*

AIR 20/1028   Board of Inquiry evidence

AIR 20/4377   RAF offensives against *Scharnhorst* and *Gneisenau*

AIR20/11351   Breakthrough of the German battleships *Scharnhorst* and *Gneisenau*: meteorological planning by German staff – English translation

CAB 106/1181   Coastal artillery action

HW 8/48   'Raiders' by Charles Morgan May 1944 (actions of German surface raiders)

PREM 3/191/20   Churchill's correspondence regarding the breakout

INDEX